Teaching
SCIENCE
With Favorite
Picture Books

by Ann Flagg and Teri Ory

S C H O L A S T I C
PROFESSIONAL BOOKS

NEW YORK • TORONTO • LONDON • AUCKLAND • SYDNEY
MEXICO CITY • NEW DELHI • HONG KONG • BUENOS AIRES

*This book is dedicated to our students at Edu-Prize Charter School,
who have inspired us to understand science through the eyes of children
and were eager yet patient as we tested and revised the activities
in this book with them.*

—Ann Flagg and Teri Ory

Book jacket from FALL IS NOT EASY by Marty Kelley © 1998 published by Zino Press Children's Books.
Reprinted by permission of Zino Press.

Book jacket from IN THE SMALL, SMALL POND by Denise Fleming. Copyright © 1993 by Denise Fleming.
Reprinted by permission of Henry Holt & Co., LLC.

Book jacket from A RAINBOW OF MY OWN by Don Freeman. Copyright © 1966 by Don Freeman.
Used by permission of Viking Penguin, an imprint of Penguin Putnam Books for Young Readers, a division of Penguin Putnam, Inc.

Book jacket from THE SONG OF SIX BIRDS by Rene Deetlefs, illustrated by Lyn Gilbert.
Illustrations copyright © 1999 by Lyn Gilbert. Used by permission of Dutton Children's Books,
an imprint of Penguin Putnam Books for Young Readers, a division of Penguin Putnam, Inc.

Book jacket from THE TINY SEED reprinted with the permission of Simon & Schuster Books for Young Readers, an imprint of
Simon & Schuster Children's Publishing Division from THE TINY SEED by Eric Carle. Copyright © Eric Carle Corp.

Produced by Joan Novelli
Cover design by Jaime Lucero
Interior design by Solutions by Design, Inc.
Interior artwork by James Graham Hale

ISBN: 0-439-22271-0

Contents

About This Book

If you were to ask your class tomorrow to make a list of five topics they would like to study and learn more about—for example, dinosaurs, frogs, space, and planes—most of the topics would be science-based. Science is hot! Now think of the one interval in your teaching day when children are relaxed yet attentive. Perhaps it is story time when you read aloud and your students sit back to listen and enjoy. This book takes the best of both worlds, literature and science, and wraps each lesson up like a gift that you can present to your students with little or no preparation.

In elementary classrooms science is often put off because there just isn't time in the academic day to cover the subjects you're required to teach. This book is a marriage of the language arts you are required to teach and the science you would like to squeeze in.

Rocket Scientists Need Not Apply

The lessons within this book are designed to support you in using literature to teach key science skills and concepts. Your role in these activities is not to be the source of all knowledge but to encourage your students to discover through experimentation. Nevertheless, each activity includes clearly worded scientific information to help solidify scientific principles in your mind so you can guide students toward a satisfying knowledge. Even if you don't feel qualified to teach science, you'll close the lesson feeling confident and competent.

A Little Mess Goes a Long Way

Research in science education tells us that children enjoy active learning; those of us who have experienced the delight of teaching hands-on science know that it is worth the mess that sometimes happens, and a little extra preparation. One way to lighten the load is to allow students to gather, set up, put away, and maintain materials. Jobs like these help children to develop a greater appreciation for classroom materials and take ownership for the appearance of their classroom. Still, we know time is valuable, so we've included activities that require a minimum of setup and cleanup.

Using Everyday Materials

Very few schools have fancy science labs or special equipment. You'll find that the materials required to teach the activities in this book are readily available at grocery stores or already in your teacher's supply cabinet. You won't need a lab, either—just desks or tables with room to work.

Managing Student Activity

Students actively engaged in science tend to move about the room and talk to their classmates. Noise is unavoidable, but it can be productive. We often explain that real science noise is welcome, but when a student moves from "serious science" into the "goof-off zone," it's time to take a break and refocus.

Once your students get their hands on the science materials, it is almost impossible to regain their attention to give further instructions. So, introduce your lesson away from the materials. (Lessons begin with a read-aloud, making it easy to pull students together and keep their attention.) Once you launch the related science investigations, you'll find it easier to speak with small groups or individuals to redirect attention or give further instructions. Great small-group conversation starters include, "Describe what happened," "Explain what you're thinking," and "What is most interesting to you?" Remember: Focus from large groups to small groups for stress-free management.

Raising the Standard

We used to paint our own picture of what children should know and be able to do in science. Now, thanks to the National Science Standards, there is a coherent vision of what it means to be scientifically literate. The Standards, put together by the National Academy of Sciences and commissioned by the Congress of the United States, describe what all students should understand and be able to do at different grade levels in various scientific disciplines. You'll know you are teaching solid science because the Standards are identified for each lesson you teach.

Throughout the book, activities will support children in developing abilities necessary to do scientific inquiry—for example, asking and answering questions, predicting, measuring, and sharing results. Because this standard applies to most of the activities in this book, it is not repeated in the National Science Standards list of connections for each lesson.

What's Inside? My Body

by Angela Royston (Dorling Kindersley, 1999)

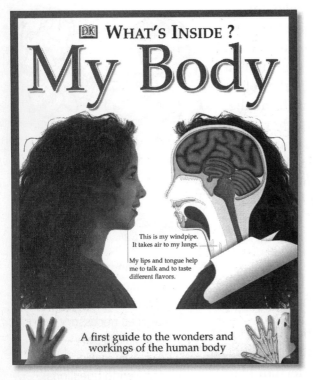

Part of the "What's Inside?" series, this clearly illustrated book satisfies a child's natural curiosity about the human body. The outside and inside of various body parts such as the eye, chest, and brain are depicted in facing pages through illustrations, photographs, and simple annotations. After you read the book aloud, your students will want to browse through it again on their own to get a close-up view of the detailed illustrations.

(This book is currently not in print, however you may find it by checking libraries, bookstores, and on-line sources.)

National Science Standards

LIFE SCIENCE

Characteristics of Organisms

☀ Organisms have basic needs, including air, water, and food.

☀ Humans have distinct body structures for walking, holding, seeing, and talking.

☀ Humans have senses that help them detect internal and external cues.

Sharing the Story

Create a two-column chart. Label one column "Outside" and the other "Inside." Have students name parts of the body and record them in the column they think they belong in. Some to include are hair, skin, skull, bones, heart, lungs, brain, nose, neck, tongue, windpipes, outer ear, eardrum, elbow, and tendons. Encourage students to confirm their predictions as you share the book. Before reading, explain that the left side of each section in the book tells about the outside of the body, and the right side tells about the inside (just like the chart children completed).

Tip

Add vocabulary for other body parts according to the interest and level of your students.

Science Notes

Nothing in the human body works alone. To make anatomy easier to understand, we study systems. The respiratory system takes in oxygen and releases carbon dioxide. The digestive system breaks down food. The circulatory system pumps blood, carrying food and oxygen to all the cells of the body. The muscular and skeletal systems hold up the body and make movement possible. The nervous system is the control center that tells all the other parts of the body what to do. It also takes in information through the senses. The outside of the body is covered with skin to keep out dirt and germs, and to help keep body fluids in. The skin has three main layers: the *epidermis* (outer), the *dermis* (middle), and the *subcutaneous* (lower). The epidermis and dermis contain the nerve endings that send signals to the brain about things we touch or that touch us.

Outside Me, Inside Me, All of Me

Students create a model of the inside and outside of the human body.

MATERIALS

* Body Card Pattern (see page 10)
* crayons
* scissors
* plastic drinking straw
* tape
* stapler

Science Vocabulary

heart: muscle that pumps blood through the body

lungs: organs that take in oxygen for breathing

stomach: organ where food goes when we eat

systems: organs of the body that work together, including the digestive, respiratory, and circulatory systems

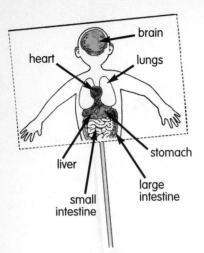

1 Copy the activity sheet on card stock. Give one to each child. Have children color in the child to represent themselves.

2 Ask students to cut out the pattern along the dashed line, then fold it in half on the solid line. Show students how to place the straw vertically inside the folded cutout, about one inch from the bottom edge. Have them tape the straw to the inside.

3 Help students staple the sides closed. (One staple to each side of the bottom is all that is needed.) Invite children to identify organs they see on the "inside" of the card.

4 Tell students to roll the bottom of the straw back and forth quickly between the palms of the hands until the inside and outside of the body appear to overlap.

SCIENCE TALK

Children may be curious about what they observed happening in step 4. The eye holds an image even after you are no longer looking at it. This phenomenon is called *persistence of vision*. The eye will hold the inside body image for a few seconds, then the outside image, and the brain will put the two views together into one to create a complete person.

All the blood in your body is contained in little tubes called *blood vessels.* If you lined up all the tubes inside one person, they would go around the Earth two and one half times!

Why do teeth get cavities?

✳ Extension Activities

So Much to Learn!

Your students may have questions that extend beyond the book. To help answer them, create a chart of questions, and stock a center with resources. Use the sample shown here as reference (see left) to make lift-the-flap record sheets. When students find the answer to one of the questions on the chart, have them write the question on the outside and the answer on the inside. Display these on a bulletin board. Students will enjoy lifting the covers to learn more about the amazing human body!

Hard-Working Heart

The heart is about the size of a closed fist and is located just to the left of center in the chest. Have students make a closed fist. When you say "lub," ask them to open their fist. When you say "dub," have them close it again. After practicing the lub-dub rhythm a few times, have them open and close their fist for a full minute. Count the number of times the fists close. (The average resting heartbeat is 90-100 beats per minute for a child.) Have students try this again for another minute, going faster or slower than the first time to approximate a normal heartbeat. Explain to your students that the heart is a muscle just like the muscles in their hand. While they can rest their aching hand, their heart pumps continuously. Have them open and close their fist as fast as they can for 15 seconds to see how much harder the heart works during exercise.

Take That Cotton Ball!

Empty a bag of cotton balls on a table. Have two students sit on opposite sides. When you say "Go!" they pick up one cotton ball at a time and place it in a basket located in the center of the table. Time how long it takes the pair to complete the task. Next, have the students don mittens and wear blindfolds. Explain that the task is exactly the same. Time them again. Discuss with the class how important our senses are in telling our brain what to do. Identify the senses used for this task.

 ## Learn More

Books

Amazing Pull-Out Pop-Up Body in a Book by David Hawcock (Dorling Kindersley, 1997). Children explore the lungs, heart, skeleton, and brain in this hands-on book.

The Children's Book of the Body by Anna Sandeman (Copper Beech Books, 1996). Breathing, eating, senses, bones, the brain, blood, and skin are presented through entertaining projects.

The Human Body: A First Discovery Book by Sylvaine Perols (Cartwheel Books, 1996). Transparent pages put a twist on learning about the workings of the human body.

The Magic School Bus: Inside the Human Body by Joanna Cole (Scholastic, 1990). Ms. Frizzle and her class are accidentally eaten by Arnold. Their journey through Arnold is a fascinating tour of the body and how it works.

What Happens to a Hamburger? by Paul Showers (HarperCollins, 1985). Watch a hamburger make its way through the digestive system. Learn how the body uses it to help make energy, strong bones, and muscles.

Software

Magic School Bus: Human Body (Microsoft): Children travel through the heart, lungs, brain, stomach, and nervous system as they explore 12 different body parts. This interactive CD includes facts and games.

My Amazing Human Body (DK Multimedia): Seemore Skinless, an animated 3-D skeleton, guides children through an exploration of their anatomy using games and activities.

Web Sites

Scholastic's Internet Field Trip: Body Surfing (**teacher.scholastic.com/fieldtrp**): Listen to a beating heart, follow blood through blood vessels, view a blood cell up close, and more—all through links at this site.

The Magic School Bus Teacher Feature (**teacher.scholastic.com/lessonrepro/results/index.asp**): Select Science and Human Body then click on "You Gotta Have Heart" for a Magic School Bus activity about measuring and recording heart rate.

Body Card Pattern

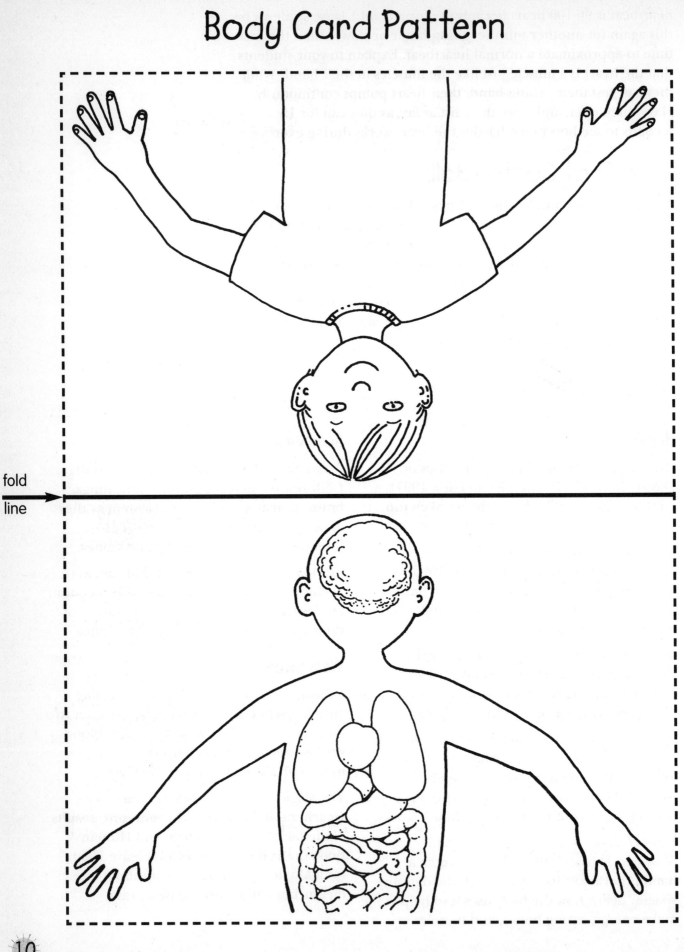

fold
line

Teaching Science With Favorite Picture Books Scholastic Professional Books

The Tiny Seed

by Eric Carle (Simon & Schuster, 1987)

Swept up in the brisk fall breeze, the tiny seed and other, bigger seeds begin a long journey, hoping to land in a favorable growing spot. But the trip is full of danger. The sun burns one seed, another falls into the ocean. Still another is lunch for a hungry bird. Even after some of the seeds land in good soil, the dangers continue. Your youngsters will be rooting for the tiniest seed to land and find a good place to grow into an adult plant that can produce seeds of its own.

National Science Standards

LIFE SCIENCE

Life Cycle of Organisms

❋ Organisms have basic needs—for example, plants require air, water, nutrients, and light.

❋ Organisms can only survive in environments in which their needs can be met.

❋ Each plant has different structures that serve different functions in growth, survival, and reproduction.

 Sharing the Story

Fill a clear plastic tumbler with water and bring it and a seed of any sort to your story circle. Get the children's attention by dropping the seed into the cup of water. Ask: *Do you think the seed will grow in the water? What do plants need to grow?* Set the cup aside and explain that *The Tiny Seed* is a book about a seed that travels and hopes to land in a great growing spot. Have the class watch for the place in the book where one seeds drops into water. Encourage them to watch for other growing spots. *Which are good? Which are not?*

Science Vocabulary

dormancy: a time when seeds do not grow

dispersed: scattered

germination: sprouting

seed: the part of the plant that contains a new, tiny plant

Science Notes

After seeds mature they are usually scattered from their parent plant. This can happen in a variety of ways. Some seeds have fluffy coatings or helicopter-type blades that enable them to be carried by the wind. Other seeds have spines or sticky coverings that can latch onto animal fur or human clothing. Animals such as bears and birds eat seeds from brightly colored berries or fruits. These seeds are not digested but are dispersed as a part of the animal's body waste. Other seeds are equipped to float on water in order to find a better home.

Seeds on the Move

Seeds float, spin, hitchhike, and even get eaten in order to find a great place to grow. Here, students experiment with ways seeds travel, then design new ways for their own seeds to travel.

MATERIALS

* plastic drinking straws
* several old tube socks
* tub of water
* "scrap" materials (foam peanuts, balloons, plastic bags, Velcro®, magnets, cotton, fabric scraps)
* glue, tape, and scissors
* reproducible record sheet (see page 16)
* sunflower seeds (in the shell; suitable for planting)

1 Prior to introducing the activity to children, set up four "Seed Stations" as follows:

* **Seed Station 1:** Place straws on a table (one straw per child). Display a sign that reads: "Use the straw to blow on your seed. Can it glide through the air and make its way to a better home?"

* **Seed Station 2:** Place a few old tube socks on a table. Display a sign that reads: "Slip the sock over your hand. 'Walk' the sock so that it is next to your seed. Can your seed stick to the sock and 'hitchhike' to a better home?"

* **Seed Station 3:** Place a tub of water on a table. Display a sign that reads: "Drop your seed into the water. Can it float to a new home?"

* **Seed Station 4:** Set out the "scrap" materials on a table along with glue, tape, and scissors. Display a sign that reads: "Use the materials to create an adaptation that will allow your seed to travel in a way that it didn't before."

2 Give each child a copy of the record sheet. Together, review what children will do to complete the sheet.

3 Give each child a sunflower seed and send groups of students off to visit Seed Stations 1-3. Have children complete the directions at each table and record results on their record sheets, then on your cue move to the next station.

4 Discuss children's results at each station. Ask: *What are the ways your seeds could travel? What ways wouldn't work? Why?* Invite students to use the materials at Seed Station 4 to design an adaption that will help their seeds travel in a way that they didn't before. Have them complete the record sheet to tell about their designs, then take their seeds back through stations 1 to 3 to see if the seeds can now fly, hitchhike, or float. Have students record results of their test, then modify their designs until their adaptation works.

SCIENCE TALK

Ask children to think of reasons a seed may need to travel away from its parent plant. (*Baby plants would have to compete with parent plants for sunlight, food, and water.*) Discuss other advantages of seed dispersal. (*It expands the area in which the plant is living.*)

Now You Know!

Witch hazel pods explode with so much force that their brown, shiny seeds fly 30 feet! What's their secret? The seeds are pointed at the end and silky smooth. When the pod bursts open it squeezes the end of the slippery seed, "pinching" it to send it flying!

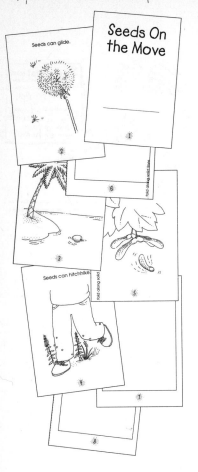

Extension Activities

Make a Mini Book

Give children copies of the mini-book on pages 17–18. Have them cut apart the pages and put them together to make books. Guide students in identifying the seeds in each picture (page 2, dandelion; page 3, coconut; page 4, burr; page 5, maple seed). Read together about the ways seeds in the mini-book travel. Can your students think of more ways? Let your young botanists complete pages six and seven to show new ways for seeds to travel, and page eight to summarize. Here are some suggestions to get your students started: *Willow seeds are lightweight and have a cotton-like puff that catches the breeze. Pinecones contain papery seeds that can flutter away in a light breeze. Ground squirrels and blue jays carry acorns away from the parent plants and bury them to be eaten later. Jewelweeds or "touch-me-nots" burst open when touched and hurl their seeds in every direction.*

Super Sprouts

The seeds in *The Tiny Seed* were not able to sprout because they landed in unfavorable places. Have students design sprouting spots like the ones in the book and see for themselves if seeds will grow. Plant a seed in a cup of soil. Water it and set it in the freezer. *Will a seed that is cold grow?* Place another seed in a cup of soil in the sunniest spot on your playground. *Will a seed that is warm grow?* Fill a cup with water and drop a seed into it. *Can a seed floating in water with no soil grow?* Be sure to water the first two seeds (cold and hot) every few days to give them every advantage. What other conditions might be interesting to test? Revisit the book for inspiration.

What's Inside?

Your students may be amazed to learn that a seed is a home for a tiny new plant. They can see this for themselves with this simple investigation. Soak dried lima beans in water for a few hours or overnight. Peel off the seed coat of the wrinkled seed. Talk about what this seed coat might be for. (*It protects the seed until proper growing conditions are found.*) Next, carefully split the seed apart at the seam. Locate the new baby plant inside. Explain that the two halves of the seed, called *cotyledons*, provide food for the tiny new plant until it can grow big enough to make food on its own. Marvel together at the many ways a seed is equipped to find a good home and then grow into an adult plant!

Lima Bean

leaves

root

seed coat

cotyledons

Seed Search

Encourage children to notice seeds in the world around them by setting up a seed-planting station in the classroom. Label a clear plastic cup for each child with his or her name. Have students fill up the cups with potting soil. Now invite children to find seeds to plant in their cups. Brainstorm places they might find them—for example, in a slice of watermelon or in a pinecone on the playground. Explain that popcorn and dried beans are seeds, too! Over the next few days encourage children to plant the seeds they find. To complement the activity, reproduce this sentence frame on the bottom of sheets of paper: _____ planted a _____ seed. Have children complete it by filling in their name and the type of seed they planted. Ask children to illustrate their sentences, then bind the pages into a classroom book and display it next to the seed cups. Some seeds will germinate and some will not. After a time you may wish to provide a lima bean seed or other surefire germinater for those children who were unsuccessful at sprouting or finding a seed of their own.

Learn More

Books

Dandelion Adventures by L. Patricia Kite (Millbrook Press, 1998). A spring wind sends dandelion seeds parachuting away to find a new home.

Ride the Wind: Airborne Journeys of Animals and Plants by Seymour Simon (Harcourt Brace, 1997). Learn more about the ways plants and animals travel with the wind.

A Seed Grows: My First Look at a Plant's Life Cycle by Pamela Hickman (Kids Can Press, 1997). Investigate facts under flaps in a fictional story about a backyard garden.

The Surprise Garden by Zoe Hall (Scholastic, 1998). Meet the seeds that yield vegetables you love to eat.

Video

The Magic School Bus Goes to Seed (Scholastic, 1995). Tour the parts of a plant and watch a seed being made.

Other

Science Mini-Books by Esther Weiner (Scholastic Professional Books, 1995). This book of ready-to-make and read mini-books includes one on plants.

The Great Seed Mystery for Kids by Peggy Henry (NK Lawn and Garden, 1993). Explore different seed types and what they need to grow with activities for grades K-6.

Web Sites

Find out more about the sunflower seeds your students worked with at these sites.

Stacie's Sunflower Page: (**www.csua.berkeley.edu/~scowan/**)

National Gardening Association (**www.garden.org**): Learn how to plant a thematic sunflower garden, and lots more.

Seeds on the Move

Seed Station 1

My seed _____ did _____ did not travel through the air.

Seed Station 2

My seed _____ did _____ did not "hitchhike" to a new home.

Seed Station 3

My seed _____ did _____ did not float on water.

Seed Station 4

❋ Design a new way to make your seed travel. Draw a picture of your design. Label the materials.

❋ How did your design work? Did your seed travel?

_____

_____

❋ How can you improve your design? Draw a picture to show how.

Teaching Science With Favorite Picture Books Scholastic Professional Books

Seeds on the Move

_____

1

Seeds can glide.

2

Seeds can float.

3

Seeds can hitchhike.

4

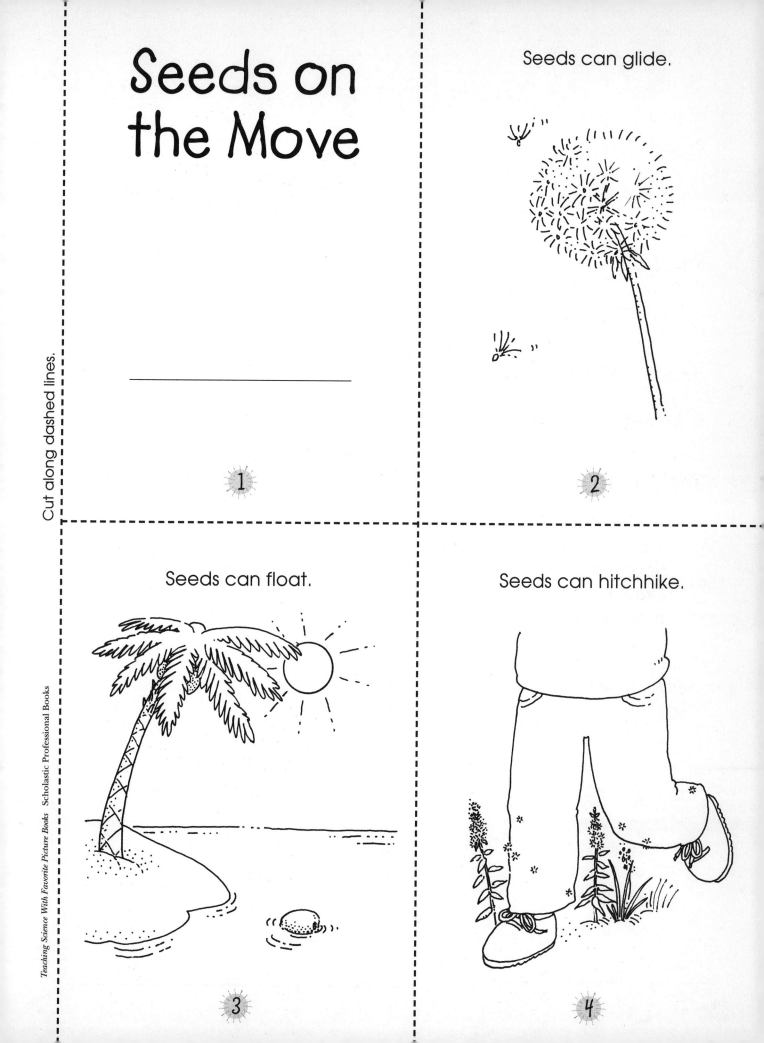

Seeds can fly.

5

Seeds can _____ .

6

Seeds can _____ .

7

Seeds get around!

8

Teaching Science With Favorite Picture Books Scholastic Professional Books

Beetle Boy

by Lawrence David (Bantam Doubleday Dell, 1999)

Gregory Sampson awakens one morning to discover he has changed into a beetle! While his family is oblivious to the transformation, his best friend Michael sees that Gregory is not himself. Although Gregory finds that being a beetle has certain advantages, he is weary when he returns home after school. When his family spots Gregory on the ceiling, they finally realize that he is a beetle. They express their love whether he is "boy or bug." When Gregory wakes the next day, he is once again a boy.

Sharing the Story

Bring in a bug (a beetle would be perfect) for students to closely examine with a magnifying glass. Ask children how their families would react if they woke up one morning as a bug. Make a chart of how life would be harder and easier. Explain that you are going to read a story about a boy who did wake up as a bug. Let them wonder aloud about how his family reacted.

Science Vocabulary

antennae: feelers used for smelling and sensing

exoskeleton: outside shell that protects an insect's organs

thorax: where wings and legs are attached

abdomen: where food is digested

Science Notes

Insects are small animals with six legs. They are protected by an exoskeleton. An insect has three body sections: head, thorax, and abdomen. There are approximately one million identified insects and up to 40 million unidentified insects in the world, which makes insects the largest animal group.

While we interchangeably use the terms *bugs* and *insects*, they are not the same. Bugs are a type of insect with special mouthparts for piercing and sucking. Many bugs look similar to beetles. Beetles, though, have mouthparts for chewing. Insects, including bugs and beetles, are considered both helpful and harmful. They are pests because they destroy crops, but they also eat other insects, such as gnats, that are annoying to people. Bugs and beetles, like most insects, can be found everywhere, living on both land and water.

Bug-a-Boos

Gregory's mom called him her "little bug-a-boo." She adored him, and your students will adore making and eating these tasty treats, which let them show what they know about an insect's body.

MATERIALS

* Insect Parts Checklist (see page 23)
* plastic bags
* pinwheel cookies
* large and small gumdrops
* large and small marshmallows
* thin black licorice strips
* pretzel sticks

✳ chocolate chips

✳ wax paper

✳ prepared icing or peanut butter (for glue)

1 Give children copies of the activity sheet. Use it to review the main parts of an insect's body.

2 Give each child a plastic bag of bug-building materials, and a sheet of wax paper for a work surface.

3 Tell students to create a bug that has all the parts listed on the checklist, using the icing or peanut butter as glue.

4 Have each student identify the insect parts by pointing to them and telling what they are (*head, eyes, antennae, wings, legs, thorax, and abdomen*). Ask students to put a check in the first column for each body part they included. When the teacher boxes on the activity sheet are checked, too, it's time to crunch and munch! (Check for food allergies first.)

SCIENCE TALK

The illustrator of *Beetle Boy* took an artistic rather than a scientific approach in creating Gregory as a beetle. Have students compare the insect pictured on the activity sheet with pictures in the book. Invite students to point out similarities and differences. Look for the body parts in the book's pictures. Can students find the head, thorax, and abdomen? The head contains eyes and *antennae*, or feelers, for sensing. The wings and three pair of legs are attached to the *thorax*, or middle. The *abdomen* is where food is digested.

✳ Extension Activities

Snug as a Bug in a Rug

Insects come in all sizes and shapes. Children will delight in perusing books on bugs. Challenge them to find unusual ones. Collect items such as clothespins, tissue paper, felt, glue-on eyes, pipe cleaners, craft sticks, cotton balls, cotton swabs, washers, buttons, and so on. Have students create bugs that show both their artistic sides and their scientific knowlege. After creating the critters, let students make up names for the new species. Use shoeboxes to design habitats, encouraging students to create environments in which the insects would be camouflaged.

Cockroaches are insects that have been around for more than 280 million years—since before dinosaurs roamed the Earth!

The Lunch Bunch

Tip

Ants have very sharp mandibles and can cause pain when they bite. Be sure children stay far enough away not to get bitten.

Who is the most unwelcome guest at a picnic? The ant, of course. *What if the ant had a choice in its picnic food? What would it eat?* Conduct an experiment to answer this question. Turn a paper plate upside down in an area where ants have been known to gather. (Avoid high-traffic areas. Place a sign near the plate that says, "Please do not disturb. Science investigation in progress.") Place one teaspoon each of a variety of items—such as fruit, seeds, bread, nuts, and sweets—around the edge of the plate. Wait about three to five minutes for the "guests" to arrive. Record the number of ants on each food. Continue the count every three minutes until there are too many to count. Then carefully help the ants off the plate and dispose of the food and the plate. Follow up by discussing students' observations during the feeding frenzy: *Did the ants stay on the plate to eat or carry the food away? Did they make a trail when they left? Where did they go? Did they cooperate or were there fights over food?*

 Learn More

Books

About Bugs by Sheryl Scarborough (Treasure Bay, 1999). Get to know more than 20 kinds of insects with the extraordinary photos and fascinating facts in this book. A parent page contains information about bugs with a facing children's page written at an early reading level.

The Best Book of Bugs by Claire Llewellyn (Larousse Kingfisher Chambers, 1998). Basic bugs such as beetles, butterflies, ants, bees, and dragonflies are introduced in this book of creepy crawlies.

Bugs! Bugs! Bugs! by Bob Barber (Chronicle Books, 1999). Characteristics of eight common insects are charted on the Bug-O-Meter in this rhyming book.

Video

Insects: The Little Things That Run the World (1989). Awesome photography brings the viewer eyeball to eyeball with butterflies, tarantulas, and bees.

Web Sites

An Ant Thology Home Page (**www.ionet.net /~rdavis/antics.shtml**): Click any cartoon ant for links to information and activities.

Ladybug Lore (**www.nwf.org/rangerrick /ladybug.html**): This Ranger Rick site contains fun and interesting facts about this tiny beetle—from how it got its name to the famous nursery rhyme.

Scholastic Internet Field Trip: Bugs Caught in the Web (**teacher.scholastic.com/fieldtrp /science/bugs.htm**): This resource provides links to several sites about cockroaches, butterflies, and general insect information.

Other

Bugs: Explore the Amazing World of Insects with this Great Activity Kit by Gerald Legg and Philippa Moyle (Smithmark Publishing, 1998). Future entomologists will find this bug kit educational and entertaining. Includes a magnifying bug jar to view live specimens.

Bug-a-Boos Insect Parts Checklist

Check each body part that you included on your insect.

Student Checklist | | **Teacher Checklist**

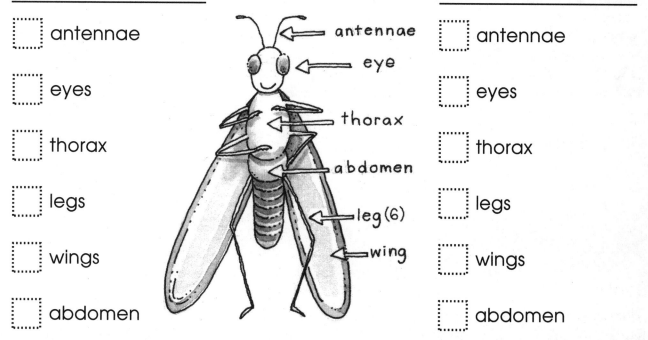

Student Checklist:
- [ ] antennae
- [ ] eyes
- [ ] thorax
- [ ] legs
- [ ] wings
- [ ] abdomen

Diagram labels: antennae, eye, thorax, abdomen, leg (6), wing

Teacher Checklist:
- [ ] antennae
- [ ] eyes
- [ ] thorax
- [ ] legs
- [ ] wings
- [ ] abdomen

Circle one insect to show what you think about the way your insect looks.

Circle one insect to show what you think about the way your insect tastes.

 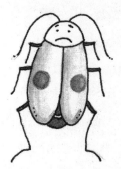

In the Small, Small Pond

by Denise Fleming (Henry Holt, 1993)

Simple rhyming text and lively illustrations provide a springboard for lots of science exploration and discussion. Each page introduces an inhabitant of a pond as the seasons subtly shift from the new life of spring to hibernation in winter. The life cycle changes of tadpoles to frogs and goslings to geese begin the book. Next a heron plunges for food, a frog chases after a minnow meal, swallows swoop up a snack, and ducks dip for delightful treats to depict the food chain. Magnificent illustrations bring the teeming environment of animals and plants in a pond to life.

National Science Standards

LIFE SCIENCE

Characteristics of Organisms

* Distinct environments support the life of different types of organisms.

Life Cycles of Organisms

* Life cycles are different for different organisms.

Organisms and Their Environment

* All animals depend on plants. Some animals eat plants for food. Other animals eat animals that eat the plants.

Sharing the Story

Create a simple mural that children can add to while you read the story to show who lives in a pond. Cut out a "pond" from blue craft paper. Place it on white mural paper. Add green paper grass around the pond and a brown paper log to the side. Copy and cut out the pond animal pictures on pages 28–29. (Make enough so that each child will have a picture.) Give each child a picture. Have children color the animals, then listen to the story. When they hear their animal's name, have them glue their picture to the mural, placing it on, over, in, or beside the pond. After reading the story, recruit volunteers to add plants such as grasses, lily pads, and cattails.

Science Notes

A pond is a small, usually shallow, freshwater habitat where many animals and plants live and grow. Ponds are usually smaller than lakes. Ponds form when low areas of land fill with rainwater, melted snow, or streams. Beavers help ponds form when they build dams in streams. Because ponds are fairly shallow, sunlight can reach the bottom, which promotes the growth of plants. Ponds are home to a variety of plants and animals that depend on each other for survival. A pond habitat supports a food chain that allows animals to thrive in the rich environment.

Science Vocabulary

habitat: a place where plants and animals live and grow

life cycle: changes in an animal from birth to death

food chain: the order in which organisms in an ecological community, such as a pond, use members as a food source

Make a Pond

Students create a pond of their own to reinforce the basic concepts of habitat, food chains, and life cycles.

MATERIALS

* ✳ shoebox with one long side removed (one for each student)
* ✳ Pond Picture Cards (see pages 28–29; copy on card stock)
* ✳ small rocks, clay, pipe cleaners
* ✳ green construction paper
* ✳ glue
* ✳ scissors
* ✳ plastic wrap (try blue for water)
* ✳ tape

Use the diorama to talk about life cycles. Have children look for examples of baby and adult animals. They should easily identify tadpoles and frogs and goslings and geese. Discuss how these animals change as they progress through the cycle from babies to adults.

1. Give each child a shoebox. Have children position the shoebox so that the cutoff side is the top and the remaining long side is the bottom.

2. Brainstorm ways to use the materials (the animal pictures, rocks, clay, etc.) to create a pond habitat—for example, by sticking pipe cleaners in bits of clay and placing them around the pond, then gluing birds on top to make them "fly."

3. As children get started on their dioramas, encourage them to be creative, using the materials to bring pond plants and animals to life.

SCIENCE TALK

A pond is a good home because it provides water, food, and shelter. Ask students what materials in their dioramas represent the water. Encourage children to identify the food each animal could find in the pond habitat. Plant eaters (*herbivores*) include tadpoles and minnows. Meat or animal eaters (*carnivores*) include turtles, frogs, swallows, and herons. Animals that dine on both plants and animals (*omnivores*) are fish, ducks, and raccoons. Discuss some of the ways animals find shelter in the pond habitat. How can this help keep them safe from predators?

✳ Extension Activities

Who, What, Where

Write the following sentences on sentence strips and cut them into three sections to show *who*, *what*, and *where*. Let students put the three parts together to heighten awareness of inhabitants of the pond as well as to reinforce language skills.

The tadpoles   wiggled and jiggled   in the pond.

The turtles   dozed   on the log by the pond.

The herons   plunged   into the pond.

The crayfish   clicked their claws   on the bottom of the pond.

The ducks   dipped   into the pond.

The raccoon   splashed its paws   into the pond.

The frog   slept during the cold winter   beneath the pond.

Pond water is often covered with a filmy layer of scum. That scum is part of the habitat and contains insect eggs that float on the surface.

Walking on Water

Cut whirligig-like shapes out of aluminum foil and float them in a container of water. Then explore surface tension with your students. Explain that *surface tension* is what lets the whirligig float on the water. Add a drop of liquid detergent to the water to break up the surface tension, and...bye-bye whirligig!

Looking at Pond Life

If you live near a pond, plan a field trip to collect some easy-to-find microscopic critters. For this activity a pond can be defined as any small, standing body of water. Even a large puddle that has been standing on the playground for several days may contain organisms. (Be sure you have permission to visit the pond and collect samples. Always watch children carefully around water.) Take along several wide-mouth jars and a long-handled fishnet. Scrape along the edge or bottom of the pond to collect samples of scum. Back in the classroom dump the scum out on a white polystyrene tray. Let children take turns using a hand lens, magnifying viewer, or microscope to locate small, moving organisms. For a challenge, try to identify pond creatures using illustrated charts or other field guides.

Some animals, even small ones, can bite or sting. Caution students not to touch organisms they find and to be sure to wash their hands after the activity.

Learn More

Books

Beaver at Long Pond by William T. George and Lindsey Barrett George (HarperCollins, 2000). Children learn about nature and pond life as they follow Beaver each evening as he leaves his lodge in search of food.

Dig Hole, Soft Mole by Carolyn Lesser (Harcourt Brace, 1996). A star-nosed mole journeys underground and underwater to a beautiful pond. On his way he encounters a variety of pond inhabitants.

One Small Square: Pond by Donald Silver (Freeman, 1994). Detailed illustrations and information invite readers to explore plants and animals that live in, on, above, and around a pond.

Pond Year by Kathryn Lasky (Candlewick, 1997). The life of a pond over the course of a year is viewed through the eyes of two best friends.

Web Sites

Bill Nye's NyeLab Episode Guide #90: Lakes and Ponds (**www.nyelabs.com/teach/eg_print /eg90.html**): Check here for basic information about lakes and ponds.

Nye Labs Home Demo #06: The Name's Pond, James Pond (**www.nyelabs.com/homedemos /printable/demo06.html**): Follow the steps to build a waterscope for viewing underwater.

The Amazing Adaptable Frog (**www.exploratorium.edu/frogs**): Topics include evolution, color and camouflage, and life cycles. Information is enhanced by video and sound links.

The National Wildlife Federation (**www.nwf.org**): Links to various sites include "Frogs Forever," which discusses the effects of environmental changes on frogs and humans.

Pond Picture Cards

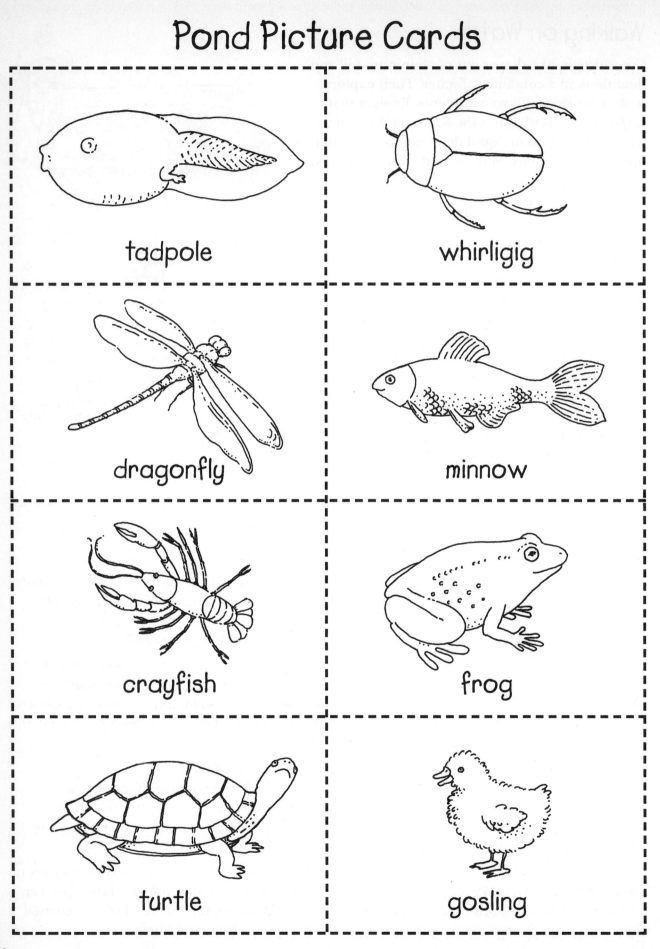

tadpole

whirligig

dragonfly

minnow

crayfish

frog

turtle

gosling

Teaching Science With Favorite Picture Books Scholastic Professional Books

Pond Picture Cards

swallow

duck

goose

heron

raccoon

muskrat

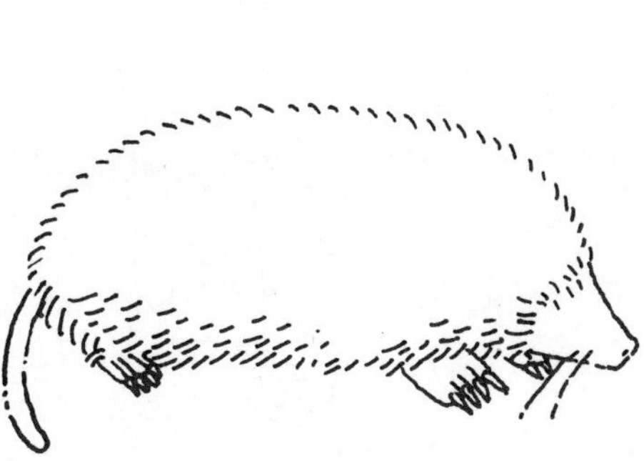

mole

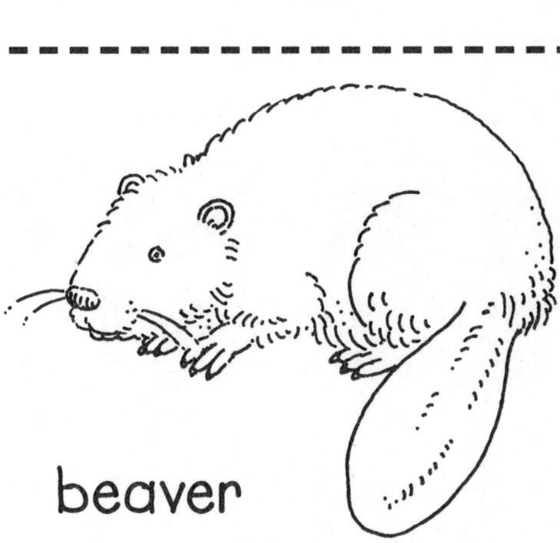

beaver

Armadillo Ray

by John Beifuss (Chronicle Books, 1998)

Armadillo Ray liked to explore his desert home at night. He was fascinated by the changing shapes of the moon. An inquisitive fellow, he asked other desert dwellers to explain the changes in this "magic thing in the sky." "What is the moon?" he asked the snakes, a prairie dog, and a grouse. Each replied with fanciful claims that the moon was related to their species. Then a wise owl told him the most unbelievable story of all—the truth. The last section of the book contains a factual explanation of the moon as well as legends from around the world.

National Science Standards

EARTH AND SPACE SCIENCE
Objects in the Sky

☀ The sun and moon have properties, locations, and movements that can be observed and described.

☀ The moon moves across the sky on a daily basis, much like the sun.

☀ The observable shape of the moon changes from day to day in a cycle that lasts about a month.

Sharing the Story

Before reading the story, ask students to draw and color a scientist-like drawing of the moon, leaving space for words on both sides. Have them add the title "Moon," then share their pictures. Guide students to notice different phases that are portrayed in the pictures. Play "My Turn, Your Turn," sharing a fact about the moon, then inviting students to do the same. Have them record facts beside their drawings, drawing lines from the moon to each fact to create a web. Now, turn off the lights and "turn on the moon" (using flashlights) as you share the cover of the book. Lights on as you encourage students to listen for the various answers Ray heard each time he asked, "What is the moon?"

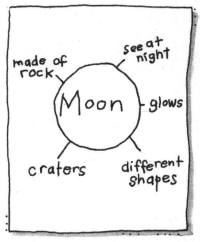

Science Notes

The moon orbits Earth once a month (about every $29\frac{1}{2}$ days). It is made of dry, dusty rocks. The "man in the moon" is actually the shape of mountains, plains, and craters (caused when meteors hit its surface). Earth orbits around the sun. The light on Earth and the moon comes from the sun. Sunlight hits the moon and *reflects*, or bounces off. At times the moon can resemble a large round ball, half a ball, or a thin crescent shape. This is caused by the movement of the Earth and moon through space. When the moon is in Earth's shadow, only part of it can be seen.

A Ray of Understanding

MATERIALS

* Armadillo Pattern (see page 34)
* crayons or colored markers
* scissors
* glue
* craft sticks
* construction paper

Science Vocabulary

reflect: bounce off something

phases: changes

1 Have students color and cut out the mask pattern. Help them make masks by cutting out the eyes and gluing the head to one end of a craft stick.

2 Cut a circle from construction paper. Set the circle aside and place the remaining construction paper on an overhead projector. Turn on the projector. Explain that the light from the projector will be the sun.

3 Ask students to imagine that the circle they see projected is the full moon. Have students hold their masks over their faces as they observe the full moon.

4 Now use the paper circle to represent Earth. Slowly move it over the cut-out circle on the overhead to block the sun and demonstrate the phases of the moon that Armadillo Ray sees. Again, have students hold up their masks as they observe the moon.

5 Reread the section of the story in which the owl answers Ray's question. Have students add this new fact to their moon web. (See Sharing the Story, page 31.) Have students use their masks to retell the story. For additional props, they can color and cut out pictures of the moon and tape them to craft sticks to use in their retellings.

SCIENCE TALK

Ask students if they saw the moon the previous night. Draw a picture of it on the chalkboard. Invite students to tell what phase they think will come next and why. Can they find the same moon shape pictured in the book? Follow up by inviting students to wonder why the moon seems to glow. (*The moon has no light of its own; it reflects the light that comes from the sun. As Earth moves between the sun and the moon, less light is reflected off the moon because Earth is in the way. This is what causes the moon to appear to change shape.*)

 Extension Activities

A Month of Moons

Number the backs of 30 white paper circles 1-30. Assign a different student to go outside with a family member each evening at an hour when you know the moon will be visible. Send home a circle and instructions to use a black crayon to shade part of the paper

Tip

While it is perfectly safe to look at the moon, students should be cautioned to NEVER look directly at the sun as its rays can damage their eyes.

Now You Know!

If you could stand on the sun and look at the moon, the moon would always appear full.

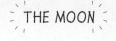

look like the part of the moon the student sees. Continue until all 30 are shaded. Display the circles in order. Guide students to discover the pattern the moon shapes make. Help them see that the moon completes a cycle about every 29 days. To go further, introduce moon vocabulary. As the reflected light from the moon becomes smaller and smaller, the moon is *waning*. As it grows larger and larger, the moon is *waxing*. By observing the moon over several evenings, students can determine if it's a waning or waxing moon.

This Rocks!

Use a small round rock to demonstrate both moon phases and reflected light. Turn off the lights and turn on a flashlight. Shine the light on the rock to model a full moon. Explain that the flashlight is like the sun. When it shines on the rocky moon, light is reflected back to our eyes. Hold the flashlight steady, but move the rock through "space" (slightly to the left and right) to show that different amounts of the moon are illuminated.

Tip

Check the moon each evening (or consult the newspaper) to ensure a continuous progression through a moon cycle. Students who are unable to get a moon reading at home can check web sources. (See Learn More, below.)

Learn More

Books

Aurora: A Tale of the Northern Lights by Mindy Dwyer (Alaska Northwest Books, 1997). A young girl named Aurora lives in the land of perpetual light. She follows the caribou in an attempt to discover darkness. On her journey she collects colors from the sky, which she uses to create the Northern Lights.

Papa, Please Get the Moon for Me by Eric Carle (Simon & Schuster, 1986). A young girl wants to play with the moon. Her father solves the problem of how to get the hard-to-reach, enormous moon home for her. The phases of the moon are revealed in Carle's trademark collage illustrations, which include several spectacular foldouts.

The Star Gift by Flavia and Lisa Weedn (Cedco Publishing, 1998). This tender, inspirational story illustrates that kindness is always rewarded. A young girl gives away everything she has to others. The stars fall from the sky and lead her to a family and love.

Why the Sun and the Moon Live in the Sky by Elphinstone Dayrell (Houghton Mifflin, 1977). This African folk tale tells how the sun and his wife, the moon, invite the sea to visit.

Video

Bill Nye Sampler I (Disney Educational Productions): The video contains an episode on the moon and another on outer space.

Web Sites

Scholastic's Answers to Kids' Questions About: The Moon (**teacher.scholastic.com /researchtools/articlearchives/space /moon.htm**): Dr. Cathy Imhoff of the Space Telescope Science Institute answers many basic questions about the moon.

Bill Nye's NyeLab Episode Guide #41 (**www.nyelabs.com/teach/eg_print /eg41.html**): Get basic information about planets and moons in our solar system.

Armadillo
Pattern

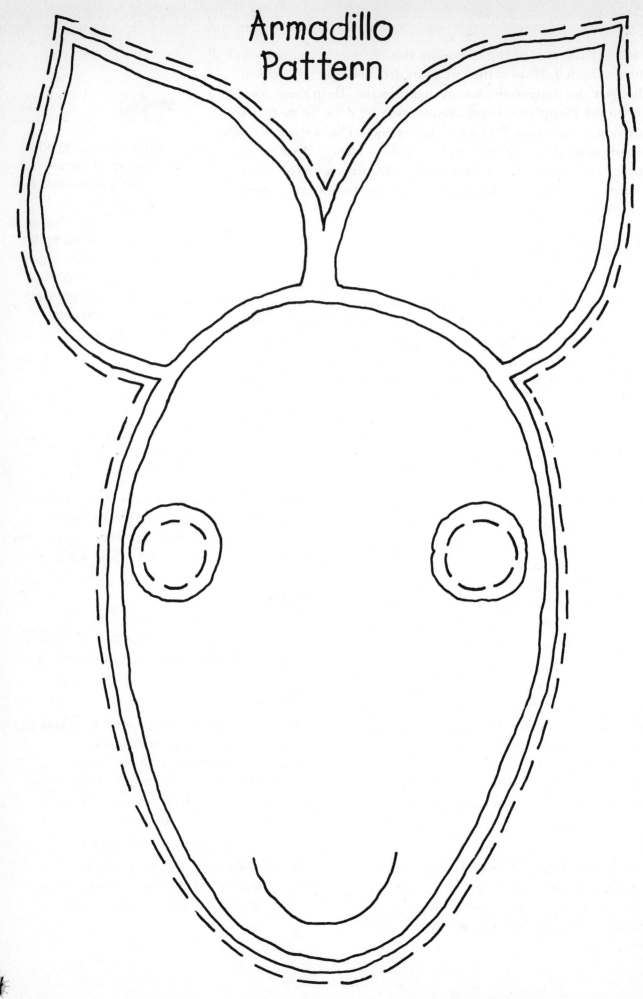

Teaching Science With Favorite Picture Books Scholastic Professional Books

Fall Is Not Easy

by Marty Kelley (Zino Press Children's Books, 1998)

National Science Standards

LIFE SCIENCE

Life Cycle of Organisms

☀ Plants have life cycles.

EARTH AND SPACE SCIENCE

Changes in Earth and Sky

☀ Weather changes throughout the seasons.

Winter, spring, and summer are depicted as "easy" seasons for a tree. In winter the tree's branches are simply bare; in spring green leaves grow; and in summer the tree basks in the warm sun. Fall, however, is not an easy season. The process of changing the colors of its leaves is challenging. As the tree struggles with the transition, it takes on a variety of delightful appearances. The book concludes where it began, with the completion of the cycle and the return of winter.

Sharing the Story

Show students the cover of the book, but hide the title. Ask: *Which season do you think is pictured here?* Let them share their guesses and reasons. Discuss how the tree will change during winter. Continue through each season. Invite students to explain why the author feels that "fall is not easy." Ask: *How might summer, winter, and spring be easier?* Tell them to listen to the author's explanation. Just for fun, invite students to identify the pictures of the tree that couldn't really happen.

Science Notes

The four seasons—fall, winter, spring, and summer—repeat in a continuous cycle. Seasons are caused by the tilt of Earth toward the sun. North America is tilted toward the sun in summer and away in winter. Seasons are opposite north and south of the equator. Summer in America is winter in Australia. Each season is about three months long. It is the tilt, *not* the distance of Earth from the sun, that causes seasons.

Deciduous trees are affected by seasons. In fall the temperature becomes colder and daylight shorter. There is not enough light for trees to make leaves, so these food-making factories shut down. The green color fades, revealing reds, yellows, browns, and golds. During winter the shortage of light and water needed for trees to make food (*photosynthesis*) causes their leaves to shed. New leaves bud during the warm spring. Summer is the perfect growing season for trees.

A Circle of Seasons Headband

MATERIALS (for each student)

- ✻ A Circle of Seasons Headband Pattern (see page 39)
- ✻ brown crayon
- ✻ watercolor paints and brush
- ✻ construction paper (a 4- by 18-inch strip)
- ✻ scissors
- ✻ tape
- ✻ glue

Give children copies of the activity sheet. Have them color the tree trunk and branches brown. They can use watercolors to paint the trees in each season.

 Adjust the length of the construction paper to make a headband to fit each student's head and fasten with tape.

3 Have students cut out the trees and glue them on their headbands in order.

4 Pair up students. Have them put on their headbands and take turns spinning slowly around while the other observes the changing seasons. (See Circulating Seasons Chant, page 38, for a chant students can recite as they spin around.)

Use white tempera paint for the snow in winter.

SCIENCE TALK

As students get ready to paint their trees, revisit the seasons illustrated in *Fall Is Not Easy*. Discuss not only the appearance of the tree, but the landscape and weather conditions, too. Use Science Notes (see page 36) to share and discuss the changes in leaves in fall, winter, spring, and summer. Discuss activities of people and animals during each season. (Students might like to include these in their pictures.) Signs of seasonal changes in cold climates include leaves dropping in fall and buds opening in spring. In warmer climates, children can observe changes in plants—for example, cacti will bloom in spring. Some produce fruit in summer.

Extension Activities

Tilting Time

Seasons are caused by the tilt of the Earth. In a darkened room shine a flashlight directly at the floor, and have students observe the *intensity*, or strength, of the light beam. Next, shine the light toward the same location on the floor, but this time hold the flashlight at an angle. The beam of light will spread out and be much weaker. Help students relate their observations to the seasons. When the Earth is tilted toward the sun, it receives direct rays of light. Let students tell what season they think it is when this happens. (*summer*)

Foliage Fun

Take a walk and have students collect five to ten leaves each. Flatten the leaves under a heavy book for a few hours. Turn the

There is no sunlight at the South Pole for 182 days each year. *Do you think there are four seasons at the South Pole? Find out!*

leaves vein-side up on a hard surface. Place white paper over the leaves and, using the sides of crayons in fall colors (reds, golds, browns, and yellows), make rubbings. Explain to students that the veins they see are the "highways" that carry water to the leaves so they can grow. Cut out the leaf pictures. Make a construction-paper tree trunk with lots of branches on a bulletin board. Let students arrange their leaf rubbings to create a fall tree that was "easy."

Circulating Seasons Chant

Winter, spring, summer, fall,
Seasons circle all year long.
Winter, spring, summer, fall,
Remember them with this song.
Winter snows on everyone.
Spring grows flowers in the sun.
Summer brings us lots of fun.
Fall drops leaves 'cause growing's done.
Winter, spring, summer, fall,
Seasons circle all year long.
Winter, spring, summer, fall,
Remember them with this song.
—Teri Ory

Learn More

Books

The Boy Who Didn't Believe in Spring by Lucille Clifton and Brinton Turkle (Dutton, 1992). Spring is just around the corner, or so two skeptical city boys keep hearing.

Frederick by Leo Lionni (Knopf, 1987). Frederick is a mouse who seems to just daydream away the summer while his friends gather and store food for the winter. He is, however, storing away poetry to warm the weary winter evenings for his friends.

Poppleton in Spring by Cynthia Rylant (Scholastic, 1999). Get to know a friendly pig named Poppleton in three stories. In the first tale he tackles spring cleaning; in the second he is overwhelmed by too many choices when purchasing a bike; in the final vignette he enjoys a spring night sleeping out in a tent.

The Reasons for Seasons by Gail Gibbons (Holiday House, 1995). See how the position of Earth in relation to the sun causes seasons.

When Autumn Comes by Robert Maass (Owlet, 1992). Color photographs tell the story of autumn arriving in rural New England.

Web Sites

Scholastic's Internet Field Trip: Spring Forward! (**teacher.scholastic.com/fieldtrp/science /springfo.htm**): This overview of spring and its impact on animal and plant life includes links to related sites.

Ranger Rick: Looking at Leaves (**www.nwf.org /rangerrick/1999/oct99/leave.html**): Click on Looking at Leaves to learn why leaves change colors.

Fingerpaint Leaf Prints (**www.eecs.umich.edu /mathscience/funexperiments/quickndirty /fingerpaint.html**): Children observe differences in the shapes, sizes, and vein patterns of leaves with an art activity.

A Circle of Seasons Headband

Color each square to match the season. Cut out the pictures.
Glue each picture on your headband in the order of the seasons.

Winter

Spring

Summer

Fall

Where Do Puddles Go?

by Fay Robinson (Children's Press, 1995)

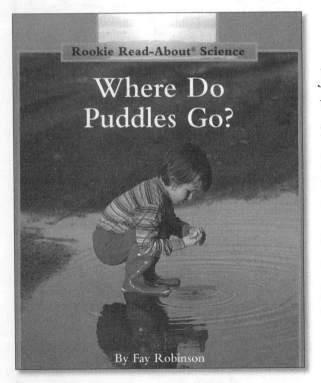

Just as the water cycle follows a pattern, so does this nonfiction book. It begins and ends with a child jumping in a puddle. The first puddle disappears into the air to form clouds. When the clouds become too heavy with water droplets, rain or snow falls to the ground and into streams and rivers, which flow into lakes and oceans. The sun causes evaporation in these giant puddles, and the water cycle repeats to make another puddle for a child's playtime.

National Science Standards

PHYSICAL SCIENCE
Properties of Materials

☀ Materials can exist in different states: solid, liquid, and gas.

☀ Some common materials, such as water, can be changed from one state to another by heating and cooling.

EARTH AND SPACE SCIENCE
Changes in the Earth and Sky

☀ Weather can be described by measurable quantities, such as precipitation.

Sharing the Story

Give students a big, raindrop-shaped piece of paper, and ask them to draw what they like to do after it rains. Inevitably, someone will illustrate splashing in puddles. Explain that they are going to learn some very big words for some very easy ideas about the interesting things that happen to those puddles they enjoy. For an appealing display, arrange the raindrops on a bulletin board under a large umbrella. Or, suspend an open umbrella from the ceiling and hang children's paper raindrops from the spokes.

Science Notes

The *water cycle* is a pattern of evaporation, condensation, and precipitation. Vital to the functioning of Earth, these processes are also at play in the everyday life of children. Puddles don't disappear after a rain; they change from a liquid to a vapor through *evaporation* when the sun warms the air. The vapor rises and meets cooler air, where it changes back into a liquid. This change is called *condensation*, and we see it as clouds. Children can see a similar change take place when they blow warm breath on a cold day. (The moisture in their breath condenses to make a "cloud.") When clouds become heavy with water droplets, *precipitation* occurs as rain or snow. These fill our rivers and streams, which flow into lakes and oceans. Water in Earth's giant puddles evaporates and repeats the cycle.

Water Cycle Simulation

Students play with water to create mini water-cycles at their desks.

MATERIALS

* ✹ Water Cycle activity sheet (see page 44)
* ✹ plastic page protector for each student (or laminate the reproducible)
* ✹ water
* ✹ blue food coloring
* ✹ small plastic cups
* ✹ straws
* ✹ toothpicks

Science Vocabulary

evaporation: the change from a liquid to a vapor

condensation: the change from a vapor to a liquid

precipitation: rain or snow

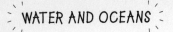

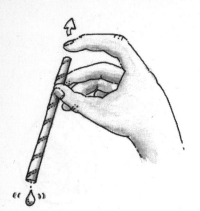

"💧"

1 Give children copies of the activity sheet and have them color the water cycle picture. Insert each picture into a plastic sleeve (or laminate).

2 Give children cups of water tinted blue. Demonstrate how to use the straw as a dropper to place one drop of water in each raindrop in panel 1, "Precipitation."

3 Using the toothpick, have children pull the drops together to form the cloud in panel 2, "Evaporation and Condensation." Let the drops adhere to form one big drop for the cloud.

4 The cloud has become too full. Pull the water droplets down into the ocean in panel 3, using the toothpick to make it "rain" again.

SCIENCE TALK

Help students understand that *precipitation* is another way to say *rain*. Ask children what kind of precipitation might fall instead of rain on a very cold day (*snow*, *hail*, *sleet*). Review the parts of the water cycle as students demonstrate them in the activity: Rain falls. The sun warms the water; it rises into the air. Droplets stick together, which students will discover as they draw the drops upward to form the cloud. Explain that the drops on their paper are not really evaporating, but students can pretend that they did, and that they condensed in the cooler temperatures to make the cloud. The cycle is completed as children pull the drops down to fill the ocean.

☀ Extension Activities

Disappearing Puddles

Give groups of students two containers with an ice cube in each. Leave one in the classroom and place the other outside in the sun. The ice cubes (solids) will change into puddles (liquids), and the puddles will evaporate. By comparing the time each ice cube takes to melt, students can observe how the warmth of the sun speeds up the process of evaporation.

Discourage students from pulling the cloud into the ocean as one big drop. Remind them that rain falls as small droplets, so they should simulate rainfall by dragging several small drops into the ocean.

If there were no precipitation, it would take 4,000 years for all the water in the Earth's oceans to evaporate.

Which One Will Condense?

Demonstrate condensation by filling one glass with tap water and another with ice cubes. Set each glass in a shallow bowl. Students will observe that water droplets form on the *outside* of the glass with ice. What's happening? Water vapor in the warm air around the glass is changing to a liquid as it comes in contact with the cold glass. Evaporated water in the air comes in contact with cooler air as it rises in the sky, making clouds. Let both glasses remain until the ice has completely melted and a puddle forms in the bowl.

 Learn More

Books

A Drop Around the World by Barbara Shaw McKinney (Dawn, 1998). A single raindrop journeys from Maine to Mumbai as the water cycle is explained through rhyming text. A teacher's guide is also available.

A Drop of Water: A Book of Science and Wonder by Walter Wick (Scholastic, 1997). Exceptional photographs complement text that teaches about evaporation, condensation, clouds, and more.

The Magic School Bus: At the Waterworks by Joanna Cole (Scholastic Trade, 1988). Ms. Frizzle and her class experience a most unusual field trip. They drive into a cloud, where the children shrink to tiny water droplets and follow the course of water through the waterworks system of the city.

See the Ocean by Estelle Condra (Ideals Children's Books, 1994). A blind girl named Nellie wins the family contest to be the first to spot the ocean on their annual trip over the mountains to their beach house. A dense fog obscures the view for her brothers, but she senses the ocean with her inner vision.

When Woman Became the Sea: A Costa Rican Creation Myth (Beyond Words Publishing Company, 1998). This Costa Rican myth explains how the seas were added when the world was made.

Software

Magic School Bus 1.0 Oceans CD-ROM (Microsoft): The Magic School Bus explores the seven ocean zones to help children learn about the sea.

Professor Iris Seaside Adventure (Discovery Store): Facts about the ocean are introduced in four languages: English, Spanish, French, and Japanese.

Video

National Geographic's Ocean Drifters (National Geographic): A newborn loggerhead turtle crawls from the sand into the ocean, where viewers follow its adventures as it encounters friends and foes.

Web Sites

Scholastic's Internet Field Trip: Exploring Oceans on the Web (**teacher.scholastic.com /fieldtrp**): Links to the Smithsonian are included on a site where students learn about different ocean ecosystems and their inhabitants.

Ranger Rick's Weird World of the Deep (**www.nwf.org/rangerrick/1998/jun98 /tdeep.html**): The world of deep sea vents is described, including the unusual means by which creatures there procure food.

Water Cycle

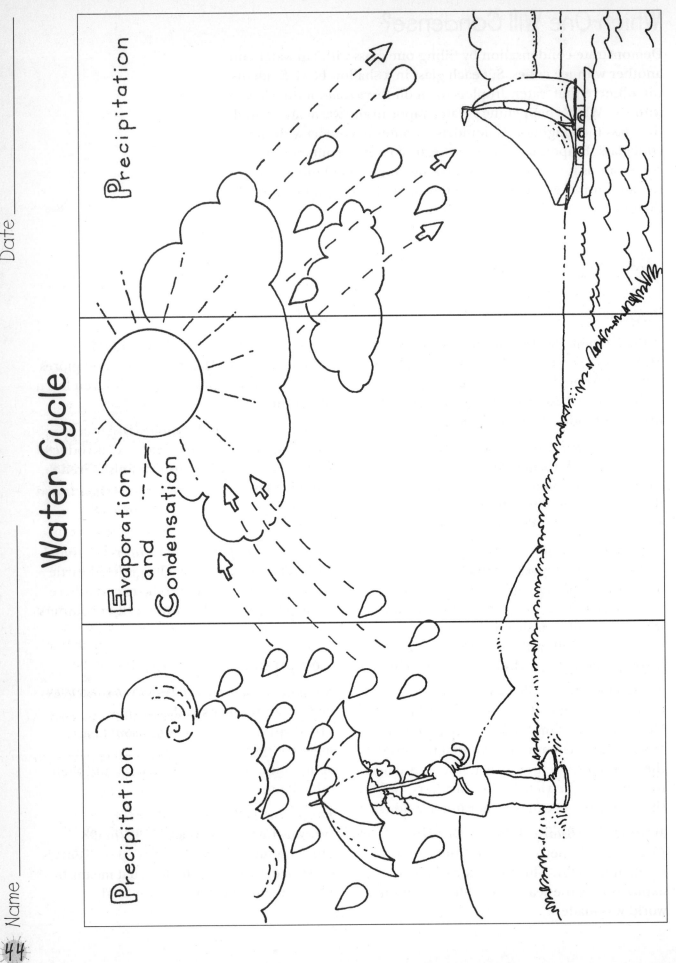

Precipitation

Evaporation
and
Condensation

Precipitation

Teaching Science With Favorite Picture Books Scholastic Professional Books

Cocoa Ice

by Diana Appelbaum (Orchard Books, 1997)

During long-ago winters in the state of Maine, ice was harvested from frozen ponds and lakes and stored in preparation for the summer months. American schooners often brought these blocks of ice and other goods to Santa Domingo to trade for cocoa and coffee beans. In *Cocoa Ice* the trading results in a long-distance friendship between a girl of the ice harvest in Maine and a girl of the cocoa harvest in Santo Domingo, and celebrates likenesses and differences of climate and culture.

National Science Standards

PHYSICAL SCIENCE
Properties of Objects and Materials

☀ Materials can exist in different states—solid, liquid, and gas.

☀ Some common materials, such as water, can be changed from one state to another by heating or cooling.

SCIENCE AS INQUIRY
Understanding About Scientific Inquiry

☀ Simple instruments, such as thermometers, provide more information than scientists can obtain using their senses.

Science Vocabulary

attribute: a quality that describes a natural part of something

solid: has shape

liquid: has no shape of its own; takes the shape of its container; flows easily

Table salt may be used to make cocoa ice, but rock salt lowers the temperature even more, and it's fun to observe. Having trouble locating rock salt? Check the canning section of the grocery store. Be sure to check for food allergies before having children taste the cocoa or cocoa ice.

✸ Sharing the Story

Display the cover of the book, read the title, and ask children to share contrasts they observe in the picture—for example, in weather, clothing, and activities. Talk about the title, *Cocoa Ice*. Ask: *What do you know about cocoa?* Have ready a half-cup of cocoa powder in a plastic cup and a toothpick for each child. Pass the cup around and invite children to dip their toothpicks into the cup and then taste the cocoa from the toothpick. Invite children to identify attributes of cocoa—for example, *powdery*, *bitter*, and so on. Finally, invite the class to listen to the story to discover the connection between dry, brown cocoa and cold, white ice.

Science Notes

Cocoa Ice introduces several concepts related to the topics of ice and snow. In the story, ice is stored in a barn that is insulated with sawdust and hay. Insulators, which also include the more familiar mittens or down-filled coat, work by trapping air. The chocolate ice that the girls in the story enjoy introduces the process of liquids changing to solids. Children will take this idea further as they make cocoa ice themselves (see Making Cocoa Ice, below), and discover that lowering the temperature of the milk mixture changes it from a liquid to a solid. Milk will freeze at approximately 27 degrees Fahrenheit. Ice can only lower the temperature to 32 degrees Fahrenheit, but adding salt to the ice further lowers the temperature and allows the milk mixture to freeze.

Making Cocoa Ice

In Santo Domingo cocoa ice is white (the cacao seed has not been roasted yet to make cocoa), but in Maine it is brown and made with ingredients much like the ones listed below. Invite children to work in pairs to create their own icy treat.

MATERIALS (for each pair of students)

✸ $\frac{1}{2}$ cup whole milk

✸ $\frac{1}{4}$ teaspoon vanilla

✸ 1 tablespoon of sugar

✸ 1 tablespoon of cocoa

✸ pint-size resealable plastic bag

* two plastic spoons
* gallon-size resealable plastic bag
* ice cubes
* ½ cup of salt or rock salt
* 2 small cups
* pair of mittens (optional)

1 Have pairs of students work together to measure the milk, vanilla, sugar, and cocoa into the pint plastic bag. Let students dip a spoon into the mixture and take a tiny taste of the liquid, then carefully seal the bag.

2 Invite students to share attributes of the mixture, such as *liquid, cold, brown chunks, flows, sweet*. Record comments on chart paper or the chalkboard, and label them "Before Ice."

3 Have students fill their gallon bag halfway with ice and add ½ cup of salt. Have them check the seal of the smaller bag one more time, then place it inside the gallon bag and seal.

4 Instruct partners to take turns shaking the bag for five minutes. Ask students if they can remember what the people from Maine in *Cocoa Ice* wore when they handled the ice. (*gloves*) Students might like to wear gloves or mittens as they shake the cold mixture.

5 When students notice that their mixtures have changed from a liquid to solid state, have them remove the pint bag and spoon out cocoa ice into individual cups. As the children enjoy the icy treat, encourage them to share its attributes—for example, *solid, brown, sweet*, and *cold*. List attributes on chart paper or the chalkboard, and title them "After Ice."

SCIENCE TALK

Review the attributes of liquid cocoa ice and solid cocoa ice. Follow up by introducing the terms *solid* and *liquid*. Guide students to recognize that *liquid* applies to the mixture before adding ice. *Solid* describes the mixture after adding ice and shaking. Extend the discussion by having children observe how the ice in the bag changed from solid cubes to a slushy liquid. Then try Salt and Ice (see page 48) to learn more about the role of salt in the freezing process.

Now You Know!

Snow and ice are both frozen water, but they are not the same. The frozen crystals in snow are mixed with a greater amount of air than are the frozen crystals of ice. Because ice is so compact, it is slower to melt than snow. Ice harvesters in Maine understood this science fact and were able to harvest, store, and trade great blocks of ice.

✳ Extension Activities

Beat the Heat

In *Cocoa Ice*, Papa and Uncle Jacob go to a great deal of trouble to keep the blocks of ice from melting because, "Ice isn't worth anything unless you get it all the way to summer without melting." Challenge your students to design an ice keeper that will beat the heat.

✳ Reread the story, asking students to notice what the men used to insulate the ice (*double-walled barns, sawdust, and hay*). Talk about conditions that influence the melting process.

✳ Divide the class into small groups. Give each group an ice cube in a small plastic container and a copy of the record sheet. (See page 50.) Have each group record the time it takes for the ice cube to completely melt.

✳ Provide a variety of insulating materials such as polystyrene, foil, paper scraps, and cotton balls. Challenge students to use the materials to design an ice keeper that will keep a second ice cube from melting as fast as the first one did. Have students discuss possible designs, then draw a sketch of their final choice on the record sheet.

✳ After building the ice insulators, give each group a fresh ice cube. Have students record the time it took for the second cube to melt, then calculate the difference.

✳ Wrap up the activity by having a "science convention." Invite each team to share its insulator and explain how it beats the heat. Let children record new ideas on their record sheets. Explain that scientists often attend science conventions to share ideas with one another.

Salt and Ice

Why add salt to ice when making ice cream? For a concrete answer that emphasizes cause and effect, try this investigation.

✳ Tell students that you would like them to do a scientific test to find out why salt is used in making ice cream. Divide the class into small groups. Give each group a plastic spoon, two plastic tumblers filled with ice, and a third tumbler filled halfway with table salt or rock salt.

✳ Explain that they will add four spoons of salt to one cup and leave the second cup as is. Instruct children to take turns adding one spoonful of salt at a time to ONE of the cups of ice, stirring after each addition.

❋ Let the cups sit for several minutes, and then have students take turns sticking their right index finger into the salt-and-ice cup and left index finger into the ice-only cup. Discuss which cup feels colder. If possible measure the temperature of each cup with a thermometer as well. You should find that the salt and ice solution is 5-10 degrees cooler, because the salt lowers the freezing point of water. This is also why oceans (salt water) don't freeze as easily as lakes (fresh water).

Food for Thought

Sugar will also lower the freezing point of water. In fact, any substance that is dissolved in water will lower the freezing point, but rock salt has a particularly dramatic effect. Repeat the experiment "Salt and Ice," substituting sugar or any other dissolvable substance for salt. Compare results for salt and sugar (or whatever substance you used). Wrap up the lesson with a delightful discussion. Ask: *Can you imagine a city that sprinkles sugar on the roadways to melt the ice?* Sweet!

❋ Learn More

Books

Ice Cream Soup by Frank Modell (Greenwillow, 1988). Two friends plan their own birthday party but the ice cream and cake will not cooperate. After making cocoa ice, children will understand what the characters forgot to do.

It's Snowing! It's Snowing! by Jack Prelutsky (Greenwillow, 1984). More than a dozen poems capture the feelings of winter.

Make Mine Ice Cream by Melvin Berger (Doubleday, 1993). A Big Book and teaching guide are also available. Call Newbridge Communications; (800) 867-0307.

Snow Is Falling (Let's Read and Find Out) by Franklyn Mansfield Branley (HarperCollins, 1986). What is snow? Is it harmful or helpful? Read all about it in this nonfiction book that contains simple experiments, too.

Video

Winter on the Farm: See how snow and winter weather affect daily farm chores and recreation in a video that is informative and magical—a winter delight!

Web Sites

Live From Earth and Mars (**it.wce.wwu.edu /necc97/poster1/WWWScience /WebWhacker/WW1.html**): This NASA-sponsored site features detailed pictures of snowflakes and answers the question, *What makes snow?*

National Snow and Ice Data Center (**www.nsidc.colorado.edu/NSIDC /EDUCATION/SNOW/snow_FAQ.html**): A teacher-friendly Q&A page answers questions such as, *Is snow edible?* and *How big do snowflakes get?*

Name _____ Date _____

Beat the Heat

Ice cube #1

_____ : _____   _____ : _____   _____ : _____
Starting time   Time melted   Total melting time

Our Ice Insulator Design

Ice cube #2 (in insulator)

_____ : _____   _____ : _____   _____ : _____
Starting time   Time melted   Total melting time

Ideas we'd try next time:

_____

_____

_____

Teaching Science With Favorite Picture Books Scholastic Professional Books

My Shadow

by Robert Louis Stevenson (Candlewick Press, 1999)

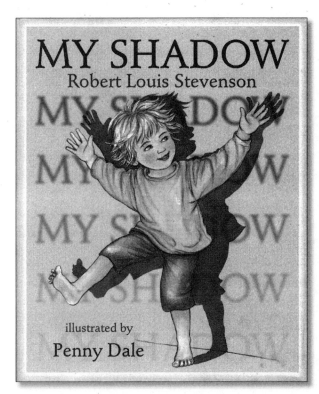

Delightful interactions of a little boy with his shadow are illustrated in this picture-book version of Stevenson's classic poem, originally written in 1885. The young child is pictured creating shadow puppets both silly and scary. He explores the changing shape and size of his shadow, and makes observations of his shadow both outside in the sunlight and in his bedroom by flashlight and lamplight. The personification of the shadow as an ever-present playmate captures the imagination of children young and old.

National Science Standards

PHYSICAL SCIENCE

Position and Motion of Objects

☀ An object's motion can be described by tracing and measuring its position over time.

Light

☀ Light travels in a straight line until it strikes an object. Light can be reflected by a mirror, refracted by a lens, or absorbed by an object.

Science Vocabulary

shadow: partial darkness within a space from which light rays are blocked by an object

light: a form of energy that makes vision possible

☼ Sharing the Story

Gather your students for story time. Without saying a word, take out a flashlight and shine it on your hand. (Position your hand between the light and a wall.) Tell students to notice the hand shadow formed on the wall. Invite a volunteer to move the light source close and far, then high and low, as you wiggle your fingers to and fro. Discuss shadows together, guiding students to understand that shadows are places of darkness created when something blocks light. Hold up the book and let the children tell you the topic of the day's story—shadows!

Science Notes

If you turn on a flashlight in a dark room and shine the light on the wall, it seems to hit it instantly. That's because light travels at a very high speed (186,000 miles per second). Light travels in a straight line, but it can be bent, or *refracted*, when it travels through certain materials, such as water or a lens. When light hits an object it can be *reflected* (as with a mirror), it can *pass through* (as with glass), or it can be *absorbed* (as with a tree). When an object absorbs light, it blocks light from passing through and a shadow results. The direction and the shape of a shadow will change as the position and angle of the light source changes. When the sun rises, shadows are long and point to the west. When the sun sets, the shadows are also long but point to the east. When the sun is directly overhead, the shadow that is formed is very small.

Investigating Our Shadows

Students trace the shadow of a stationary object over time to make connections between the sun's position and the shadow it makes.

MATERIALS

- ☼ Investigating Our Shadows activity sheet (see page 56)
- ☼ scissors
- ☼ glue
- ☼ chalk
- ☼ masking tape

1 Use the reproducible as a predicting activity before going outside with students. Give each child a copy. Ask: *Which shadow do you think goes with early morning? midday? late afternoon?* Have children draw a line to the pictures to show their predictions.

2 Go outside on a bright and sunny morning to a safe, paved area that receives full sunlight through the day. Invite children to move and play with their shadows.

3 Regroup by having children each sit with a partner. Give each team a piece of masking tape and a piece of chalk. Have each team spread out and make an X with a piece of masking tape somewhere on the pavement. Have one child stand on the X while the partner draws a chalk outline around the shadow cast. Have the teams measure the length of the shadow, then write their names and the time of day inside the outline. Before returning to the room, notice the position of the sun in the sky. Have children cut out the picture that most closely resembles their shadow and glue it in the appropriate space.

4 Repeat the activity at noon and again just before the end of the day. Each time have students repeat step 3 to draw a total of three chalk outlines during the day. Have them notice and record the location of the sun and complete their record sheets.

5 Compare children's predictions with their results. Now, help children think about their shadows like clocks: *Could they tell the time (approximately) by looking at their shadows? Why?*

SCIENCE TALK

Guide a discussion to help children make a connection between the position of the sun, the time of day, and the size and direction of their shadows. (*The length and direction of the shadow depends on the position and angle of the light source.*) Begin by asking: *What is the light source outside? What is blocking the sun to make our shadows?* Have students share observations of the sun's changing position in the sky, and then discuss how the position of their shadows changed. Make similar observations about the length of their shadows. Ask: *When was it the longest? shortest?* Have students compare their shadows. Is everyone's shadow the same length? Why not?

Remind children not to look directly at the sun as this may cause damage to their eyes.

Children often believe that the sun moves while the Earth remains still. The expression "the Sun rises in the east and sets in the west" seems to reinforce this thinking. Young children are not able to grasp that Earth's rotation sets the schedule for the sun "rising" and "setting" each day (to make "day" and "night"), but you can use the activity Investigating Our Shadows to lay a foundation for a deeper understanding as they grow and continue to explore related concepts.

Extension Activities

Mystery Shadows

Create a large white area on a wall with white bulletin-board paper, a white board, or a slide screen. Gather a collection of small objects that make interesting shadows, such as scissors, a die-cut shape, or a paper clip. Hide the mystery items in a box. Position the overhead projector so that it shines on the screen. Use a piece of cardboard to create a barrier around the overhead so that students cannot see the object. Darken the rest of the room. Gather children on the floor between the projector and the screen. One at a time, lay a mystery item on the glass top of the projector so that it casts a shadow on the screen. Position the object in different ways to create interesting shadows and give a variety of views. Have students raise their hands to identify the object from the shadow it projects. Children will enjoy taking a turn choosing and projecting the shadows, too, while their classmates guess.

Shadow Play

Go outside on a sunny day for a game of "Shadow Tag." Explain to players that the person who is "It" can tag them only by stepping on their shadows. Once tagged, children must stand completely still (try freezing in interesting positions to make interesting shadows) until everyone is caught. Challenge children's thinking about shadows by asking: *Is it easier to be "It" and play Shadow Tag at noon or in the late afternoon?* (In the afternoon because the shadows are longer and easier to catch.)

Shadow Me

Pair up students and explain that they are going to take turns being their partner's shadow by imitating everything their partners do. Demonstrate before you begin. Ask a student to stand facing you and slowly move to strike a pose while you copy the exact movement and end up in the same pose. Have students try it themselves, starting slowly so that the "shadow" can keep up!

Sun Dials

In the activity "Investigating Our Shadows," the children's shadows were like a sundial—the size and position of the shadow were a direct result of the time of the day and the position of the sun. Lots of different materials can be substituted for a more scientific version of the activity. The two necessities are a flat surface and a vertical object. A long nail hammered into a flat

Now You Know!

The planet Venus shines brightly enough to create shadows on white surfaces when it is a clear, dark, moonless night.

piece of plain wood works well. If desired, turn the wood into a sundial by painting a 12, 3, 6, and 9 on the board like a clock face. Before setting it up outside, use the board in a darkened classroom with a flashlight simulating the sun. Cover the end of the flashlight with a piece of cardboard in which you've cut a small opening to narrow the beam. Put the "sun" in the east, low on the horizon, and observe the shadow. Move the "sun" slowly overhead and watch the shadow change. Let the "sun" set in the west and notice the direction of the shadow. Take the sundial outside in a sunny location and check the shadow at regular intervals. Ask: *Is this an accurate way to tell time? How could we make it more accurate? Should we rewrite the numbers on the sun clock?* Find out more about sundials. (See Learn More, below, for a web site suggestion.)

# Learn More

Books

Guess Whose Shadow by Stephen R. Swineburne (Boyds Mills Press, 1999). An array of photographs invites readers to guess the origins of shadows.

No Mirrors in My Nana's House by Ysaye M. Barnwell (Harcourt Brace, 1998). There are no mirrors in her Nana's house to reflect a young girl's poverty, allowing her instead to see love and beauty. Based on a black gospel hymn, the book's message is that children can rise above their environment.

Nothing Sticks Like a Shadow by Ann Tompert (Houghton Mifflin, 1988). Rabbit attempts to win a bet with Woodchuck that he can get rid of his shadow. Despite the assistance of his many animal friends, he is unsuccessful— until nightfall.

The Rainbow Fish by Marcus Pfister (North-South Books, 1992). Iridescent fish scales glitter in the light as the lonely Rainbow Fish gives away his beautiful scales to win friends. The lesson that beauty is what we have inside us is the moral of this lovely story.

Shadow by Marcia Brown (Scribner, 1982). The eerie, haunting image of Shadow is revealed in this story based on a poem of Africa. The shifting, dancing Shadow appears wherever there is light and fire.

Teddy Bear Tears by Jim Aylesworth (Atheneum, 1997). A young boy reassures his teddy bears that their bedtime fears are groundless.

Web Sites

Fish Tank Optics: Learning How Light Travels (**www.eecs.umich.edu/mathscience /funexperiments/agesubject/subject.html**): This lesson plan gives clear background facts about light as well as several activities.

Bill Nye's NyeLab Episode Guide #27: Light Optics (**www.nyelabs.com/teach/eg_print/eg27.html**): Basic information about light optics is presented.

Introduction to Shadows (**www.owu.edu /~mggrote/pp/physics/c_introduction.html**): Basic shadow theory is explained through simple activities and questions.

Sundials (**www.owu.edu/~mggrote/pp /physics/c_sundials.html**): Get detailed instructions for creating a sundial from simple materials.

Shadows (**www.exploratorium.edu/snacks /shadows/index.html**): A simple demonstration reveals the importance of the relative positions of light sources, screens, and the object casting the shadow.

Investigating Our Shadows

Cut out the picture that matches your shadow each time. Glue it in place.

Early Morning

Time: _____

Our shadow is _____ long.

Midday

Time: _____

Our shadow is _____ long.

Late Afternoon

Time: _____

Our shadow is _____ long.

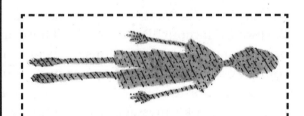

Teaching Science With Favorite Picture Books Scholastic Professional Books

A Rainbow of My Own

by Don Freeman (Puffin Books, 1966)

When a small boy observes a rainbow outside his window, he runs out to catch it. When he cannot reach the elusive rainbow, his imagination takes over. He wonders what it would be like to have his own rainbow to play with. The boy discovers the colors of rainbows in the flowers in his garden. When he returns home, the sun is shining through the water in his goldfish bowl, creating a beautiful rainbow of his own in his room. Don Freeman blends fantasy and reality as both the wonder and science of rainbows are explored.

National Science Standards

PHYSICAL SCIENCE

Properties of Objects and Materials

❋ Objects have many observable properties, including color.

❋ Light can be refracted or absorbed by an object.

☀ Sharing the Story

Before reading *A Rainbow of My Own* with children, invite them to share experiences and information about rainbows. Talk about the colors they've noticed in rainbows. Invite them to share places they have seen rainbows other than in the sky. Ask them to listen carefully for all the places the boy in the story finds rainbows.

Science Notes

For a rainbow to occur, light needs to pass through a prism. The light is provided by the sun, and the prism is furnished by the water droplets suspended in the air after a rain. Light is bent as it passes through the water droplets, and the colors of the spectrum become visible. The colors will always occur in the same order: red, orange, yellow, green, blue, indigo, and violet. The acronym ROY G BIV can help children remember the order. (Some scientists say that indigo should not be included because it cannot really be seen between blue and violet.) Just as light can be separated to reveal an array of color, so can pigments through a process called *chromatography*. The science of rainbows contains concepts that are difficult for young children to grasp. Activities that follow will give children experiences separating and mixing colors to create a different kind of rainbow of their own.

Tip

Prisms are often difficult to use with children. Diffraction grating glasses are a wonderful, easy alternative. Visit **www.rainbow symphony.com** *for ordering information. Your entire class will see the light!*

Science Vocabulary

chromatography: the process of separating pigments

rainbow: curved band across the sky revealing the spectrum of colors in light

spectrum: colored bands formed when light is bent

Rainbow Ring

With just three colors, children will create a ring of many colors. You can plan to have students work independently or with partners in this activity.

MATERIALS

- ☀ Rainbow Ring activity sheet (see page 61)
- ☀ plastic sleeves (or a clear transparency)
- ☀ three small jars
- ☀ red, blue, and yellow food coloring
- ☀ water
- ☀ straws (to use as droppers)
- ☀ toothpicks
- ☀ white paper towels

1 Prepare the following color mixtures:

   ※ In one jar mix 10 drops of red food coloring with 10 drops of water.

   ※ In the second jar mix 10 drops of blue food coloring with 10 drops of water.

   ※ In the third jar mix 10 drops of yellow food coloring with 10 drops of water.

2 Have children fill one circle at a time on the Rainbow Ring activity sheet, using a straw to place one drop of color on each of the color dots. (Key: R = red; Y = yellow; B = blue)

3 Have children use a clean toothpick to mix each color-dot combination together.

4 After stirring all 12 circles, have children place a white paper towel over the template and watch the colors mix to create a rainbow of colors on the paper towel.

SCIENCE TALK

Talk about the colors children made by mixing the dots of color. Write the rainbow acronym ROY G BIV on the chalkboard. Ask: *Which of these colors did you use for the Rainbow Ring?* (red, yellow, and blue) *What colors did you make from the small circles using just red and yellow? yellow and blue? blue and red?* Explain that sunlight is also made of three main colors—red, green, and blue (RGB). After it rains, lots of water drops are in the air. When sunlight goes through the water drops, it bends and we see the colors of the rainbow.

A straw makes a great dropper. Place the straw in water. With the straw in water, bend over the top third of the straw. Squeeze the doubled part and lift the straw out of the water. Continue to squeeze the straw at the bend, releasing it to let water go drop by drop.

✳ Extension Activities

Rainbow to Go

The boy in the story finally caught a rainbow in his room. Here's how your students can capture a rainbow, too—and take it home! Prepare a "rainbow mixture" by combining $\frac{1}{3}$ cup sugar and 1 cup cornstarch with 4 cups cold water. Heat the mixture, stirring constantly, until it begins to thicken. Let it cool and divide into three containers. Add red food color to one container, blue to the second, and yellow to the third. Place a spoonful of each color into a resealable plastic bag for each student. Children will delight in squishing and squashing their rainbow colors together.

Now You Know!

If the sun is low in the sky, near the horizon, an observer on a high mountain might see the entire circle of a rainbow.

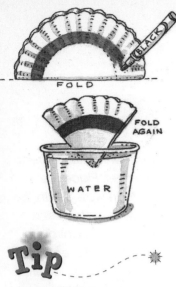

Rainbow Surprise

Create a sensation by asking children if they have ever seen a black rainbow. Then produce one right before their eyes! Fold a coffee filter in half. Use a soluble black marker to draw a rainbow-like arch on the coffee filter. (See illustration, left.) Fold the filter one more time, and place the pointed end into a glass of water so that the black arch is above the waterline. Have children gather around and watch the colors separate as the water reaches the black line. Surprise! Give children their own coffee filters, black markers, and cups of water. Let each child create an explosion of color from a "black" rainbow.

Tip

Raindow Surprise is a chromatography activity. Different brands of black markers will create different chromatograms or color patterns. Another variation is to use different colors of markers.

Capture a Rainbow

Invite children to "capture" rainbows with a bottle of bubbles. Take students outside on a sunny day. Bring along several bottles of bubble-making liquid and some bubble wands. Let children take turns blowing bubbles into the air. Children not blowing bubbles can chase the bubbles, looking for tiny rainbows that seem to float on top of the bubbles. Where do these rainbows come from? Water droplets in the bubbles act as a tiny prism that bends or *refracts* the light, breaking it up into the different colors of the spectrum—and creating a rainbow.

Learn More

Books

Little Blue and Little Yellow by Leo Lionni (Mulberry Books, 1995). A tale of two young friends teaches color concepts.

The Magic School Bus Makes a Rainbow: A Book About Color by Joanna Cole (Scholastic, 1997). Ms. Frizzle and her class learn about colors and light as the school bus takes them on a journey inside a pinball machine.

Mouse Paint by Ellen Stoll Walsh (Voyager Picture Book, 1995). Explore the science of primary colors, secondary colors, and color mixing as three little mice splash about with their paints.

Planting a Rainbow by Lois Ehlert (Harcourt Brace, 1992). A mother and child plant a family garden that grows into a brilliant rainbow of colorful blooms.

Rain by Robert Kalan (Mulberry, 1991). This easy-to-read book with predictable, repetitive language teaches young children about colors, rain, nature, and rainbows.

Web Sites

Colorworm Explains Color (**www.cs.iupui.edu /~pellison/colorworm/home.html**): This online book includes information on an assortment of color topics.

Cyberhaunts for Kids/Science/Learn About Rainbows (**www.unidata.ucar.edu/staff /blynds/rnbw.html**): Find simple and complex information about rainbows here.

Elementary Science Program Homepage: Investigating Color (**www.monroe2boces.org /shared/esp/color.htm**): Three easy science investigations help children learn about color.

Rainbow Ring

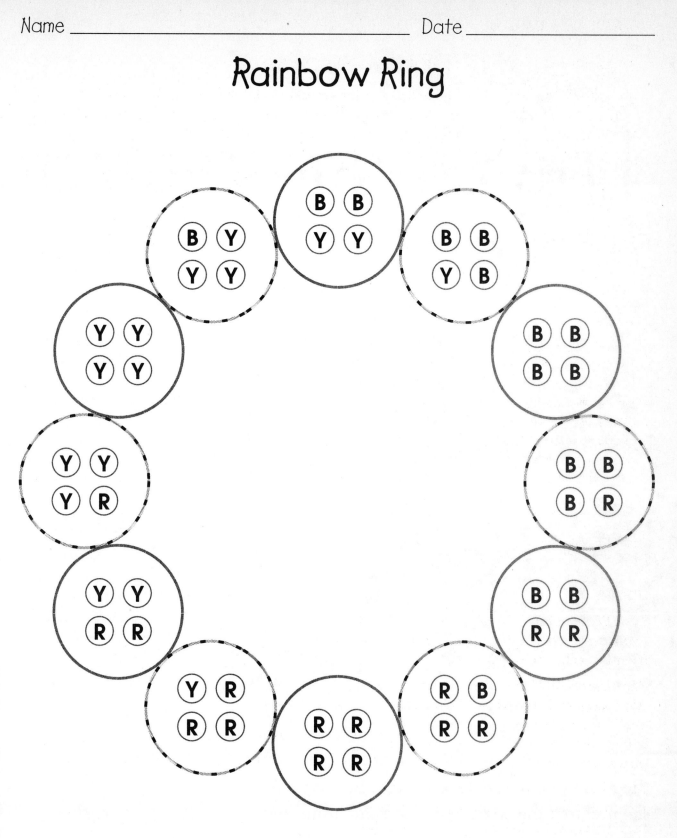

Teaching Science With Favorite Picture Books Scholastic Professional Books

The Grumpalump

by Sarah Hayes (Clarion, 1990)

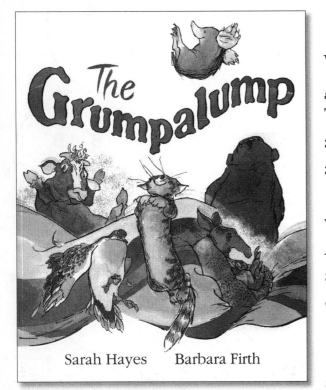

What is a *grumpalump*? That's what all of the animals in *The Grumpalump* want to know. A chain of animals climb on the "grumpalump." (It seems to be a brightly colored pile of fabric.) Each animal has its own reaction to the lump: The bear stared, the cat sat, the mole rolled, the dove shoved, but not one seemed to know what to do with the lump that grumped. The gnu, however, blew and the "grumpalump began to grin" and then became a large, inflated hot-air balloon that flew away, gnu and all.

National Science Standards

EARTH AND SPACE SCIENCE

Properties of Earth Materials

* Earth materials are solid rocks and soils, water, and the gases of the atmosphere.

* Earth materials have different physical and chemical properties that make them useful in different ways.

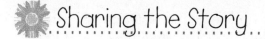

Sharing the Story

Introduce *The Grumpalump* with a riddle: *You can't see me, smell me, or taste me, but I am all around you. What am I?* (air) Tell students that *The Grumpalump* is a book that contains a kind of riddle, the answer to which is "air." Share the cover, and explain that all of the animals pictured will try to figure out the identity of the colorful lump they are sitting on. Before beginning the story, invite students to offer their own suggestions. Record their ideas.

Science Notes

We cannot see, smell, or taste air, but air is all around us. Air is made up of many invisible gases that extend from the surface of Earth into outer space. A gas is something that has no shape of its own but spreads out to fill up whatever space it is in. It can fill a space as large as the room you are in or as small as a bubble in your bubble gum. Why is air important? Air contains oxygen, which is essential to all living things. Air shields us from the sun's harmful rays. Air traps heat from the sun and keeps living things on Earth warm. Finally, air takes up space and has weight. Balloons filled with helium or hot air can therefore rise above the earth because they are lighter than the air around them, but balloons filled with breath are not light enough to rise up.

Huff and Puff: How Much Air Is Enough?

The gnu knew what to do with the grumpalump. Have your students huff and puff their way to a grumpalump of their very own while practicing prediction skills and connecting cause and effect—all the while discovering that air takes up space.

MATERIALS (for each student)

✳ Huff and Puff Pattern (see page 67)

✳ crayons

✳ scissors

✳ masking tape

✳ a 9-inch balloon

Science Vocabulary

air: the mixture of gases that surrounds the Earth; often called the *atmosphere*

wind: moving air

breath: warm air that comes from inside the lungs

Tip

Before giving children the balloons, run through the procedure of predicting how many puffs it will take to inflate the balloon, inflating the balloon, testing it out, and repeating if necessary. (This will help them keep their attention on the directions, instead of on the balloons.)

1 Give each child a copy of the activity sheet. Have children color and cut out the pattern pieces, then tape together the ends (A and B) to make a crown-like ring.

2 Ask children to predict how many breaths it will take to inflate the balloon so that the ring will fit snugly around the middle of the balloon. Record this number on the crown.

3 Record everyone's predictions. Have children blow up their balloons (or do this for them), using the number of breaths they predicted. Pinching the end of the balloon closed, have students try the crown on the balloon. Does it fit snugly?

4 If the balloon is too large or too small, have children release all the air, then try again with a new number of puffs. Have children compare actual puffs to their predictions.

5 With their balloons now correctly inflated (tied and sitting inside the crowns), have students toss them up. *Do they fly?* (The balloons will stay up briefly, because the surrounding air resists the motion of the object traveling through it—that is, the balloon.)

SCIENCE TALK

 Let students share what they think takes up the space inside their grumpalump balloons and gives them shape. (*air*) Guide a discussion of the activity with these questions:

✳ Did everyone use the same number of breaths to fill up their balloon? (*No, because we all exhaled different volumes of air.*)

✳ How is your balloon different from the inflated grumpalump in the book? (*Somehow, the gnu's breath caused the grumpalump to rise, but our breath did not cause our balloons to rise.*)

While at rest, an adult will inhale about one-quarter pint of air, but during exercise the same adult may inhale as much as two pints of air.

Extension Activities

The Gnu Knew

The gnu in *The Grumpalump* was full of hot air! Demonstrate that hot air rises with this simple demonstration. Slide the lip of a balloon over the rim of a glass beverage bottle and let the balloon hang limply on the outside of the bottle. Set the bottle in a pan of very warm water. The hot water will warm the air inside the bottle, causing the air to expand, move up into the balloon, and inflate the balloon right before your eyes! Help children understand that for a hot-air balloon like the grumpalump to rise, it must be filled with air that is lighter than the air around it. Warm air is lighter than cool air. When the air inside a hot-air balloon is heated, the air molecules speed up and spread out. This makes hot air less dense, and therefore lighter, than the cooler surrounding air, and the hot-air balloon rises. When the children inflated their grumpalump balloons, they learned that air takes up space. Show again that air takes up space with the fascinating demonstrations that follow.

Tip

When purchasing balloons for experiments like this, look for "helium quality" balloons. These balloons are thicker and do not tear as easily.

Evidence of Air

Push an upside-down glass of water into a sink full of water, then let go. The air inside the glass makes it pop up. Blow through a straw into a glass of water. *What makes the bubbles?* Stand on a chair and drop an unfolded piece of paper. *What makes it float as it falls?*

Balloon in a Bottle

Hang a sturdy 9-inch balloon inside a 2-liter plastic soda bottle. Stretch the mouth of the balloon over the bottle's neck so that you can blow into the balloon while it is inside the bottle. Have a volunteer attempt to blow up the balloon while it is in the bottle. (For sanitary reasons, change the balloon each time you allow another volunteer to attempt to blow up a balloon.) No matter how hard they puff, your volunteers will not be able to inflate the balloon. Why? Although it is not visible, there is air inside the soda bottle completely surrounding the limp balloon. Students cannot blow up the balloon because there is no room inside the bottle for the balloon to inflate. Share this information, and then tell students that there is a way to blow up the balloon inside the bottle. Allow childen to problem-solve and try their solutions before you reveal the simple solution: Use a tack to punch a hole in the bottle! The hole will allow air to escape from the bottle as you blow new air into the balloon.

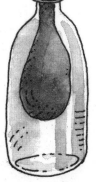

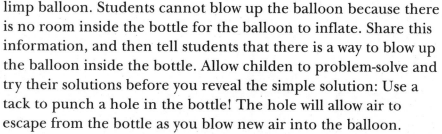

Learn More

Books

Air Is All Around You by Franklyn M. Branley (HarperCollins, 1986). Learn about the properties of air, including why it takes up space. Try the science experiments included in the book.

The Big Balloon Race by Eleanor Coerr (HarperCollins, 1984). Part of the "I Can Read" series, this book introduces readers to the balloonist Carlotta Myer's historic 1882 race.

Experiments With Air by Bryan Murphy (Lerner Publications, 1992). Looking for more ways to demonstrate the principles of air? This book has experiments and clear explanations.

Hot-Air Henry by Mary Calhoun (William Morrow, 1984). Join Henry the Cat as he sets sail in a hot-air balloon.

Michael Bird-Boy by Tomie dePaola (Prentice-Hall Books, 1975). Want to discuss air pollution? This darling book finds Michael Bird-Boy convincing a businesswoman to clean up her air-polluting honey factory.

Book and Tape Sets

What Can Air Do? (National Geographic): Learn about the wind, how it moves things, and why all living things need air to survive. This set contains a read-along cassette, 30 student books, activity sheets, and teacher's guide.

Software

I Love Science (DK Multimedia): Science topics come to life with this program's simple presentations and hands-on experiments.

Web Sites

Nova Online: Balloon Race Around the World (**pbs.org./wgbh/nova/balloon/**): See pictures of the first balloon ride ever, and take a quiz with questions such as, "How do hot-air balloons float?" A teacher's guide is included.

Kodak: Albuquerque International Balloon Fiesta (**balloonfiesta.com**): View colorful photos of hot-air balloons from this amazing annual event.

BrainPOP- Earth: Atmosphere (**Brainpop.com /science/earth**): Watch a movie and learn tons of facts about Earth's atmosphere!

NASA: Beginners Guide to Aerodynamics (**www.lerc.nasa.gov/WWW/K-12/airplane /bga.html**): This site offers information and great graphics about the principles of flight.

Huff and Puff: How Much Air Is Enough?

Predicted Puffs: _____

Actual Puffs: _____

A

B

The Song of Six Birds

by Rene Deetlefs (Dutton, 1999)

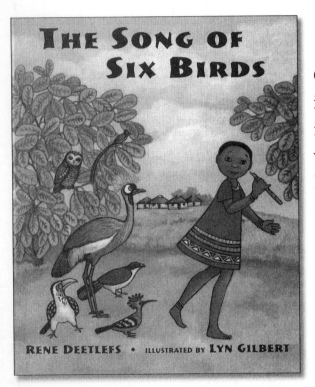

Children gain insight into life in an African village with this heartwarming tale. Lindiwe awakens one morning to discover a flute beside her bed. She is disappointed when her mother's special gift produces dreadful noises that startle the dog, frighten the chickens, and cause the baby to scream. On her quest to find music for her flute, she encounters six birds who each contribute their sound. She and the birds joyously return to her village community for a lively celebration of music and dance.

National Science Standards

PHYSICAL SCIENCE

Position and Motion of Objects

❋ Sound is produced by vibrating objects.

❋ The pitch of a sound can be varied by changing the rate of vibration.

Sharing the Story

Give each child a straw. Have children flatten one end and cut both sides to form a point, as shown. When they pinch the pointed side, place it in their mouth, and blow, irritating squawks result. Display the cover of the book. Explain that a girl was given a flute by her mother which also produced awful sounds. Invite them to listen to how she found a way to create beautiful music with her flute. (For a related activity, see The Straw Revisited, page 71.)

Tip

Children will enjoy echoing the sound made by each bird as you read.

Science Notes

Sound is a form of energy caused by vibrations. Sounds can be soft or loud (*volume*) and high or low (*pitch*). Volume is a measure of the amount of energy in sound. Loud sounds have more energy than soft sounds. Fast vibrations cause high sounds. Slow vibrations cause low sounds. A xylophone provides an excellent demonstration of pitch. The short bars vibrate quickly and produce higher sounds, and the long bars vibrate more slowly and produce lower sounds. Sound travels in waves produced by a vibrating object. It travels in every direction from the vibrating object. The waves move in a manner similar to waves caused when a rock is dropped into a pool of water.

Science Vocabulary

sound: energy that we hear

music: sounds made by the voice or by instruments that are arranged together

vibration: back and forth movement

noise: sounds, typically those that are loud, unexpected, or unpleasant

Singing Owls

Investigate sound waves by making owls that call out!

MATERIALS

* ❋ Singing Owl Pattern (see page 73)
* ❋ small disposable plastic cups
* ❋ string (about 2 feet per child)
* ❋ jumbo paper clips
* ❋ glue or tape

1 Photocopy the activity sheet on card stock for each child. Have children color and cut out the owl.

2 Make a hole through the center of the cup bottoms. You may wish to use the hot tip of an empty glue gun to sear a hole in the bottom of each cup. (Prepare these in advance of the lesson.)

3 Help children thread the end of a 2-foot-long piece of string through the outside bottom of the cup to the inside. Have them pull the string about halfway through and tie the string on the outside bottom of the cup tightly around the paper clip.

4 Gently pull the string so that the paper clip rests on the outside bottom of the cup. The paper clip will keep the string from pulling out.

5 Glue or tape the owl to the outside bottom of the cup. The owl is ready to call out. Have students wet their fingers, then gently pull down the length of the string with their fingers, using short tugs.

SCIENCE TALK

Have students tap their fingers lightly on a desk. Explain that the tapping is causing the air to *vibrate*, or move back and forth. These vibrations travel to those great sound-catchers, our ears. Next, have students pair up. Have one partner lay one ear on the desk and cover the other ear with his or her hand. Have the other child lightly tap the desk. *What's vibrating now in order to produce sound?* The desk, of course! Sound is caused by vibrations. In the Singing Owls activity, when students pull the string, it vibrates. The sound waves are bouncing back and forth inside the cup causing a nice, loud sound. Try pulling on a string without a cup. *How is the noise different?*

Now You Know!

Humans can hear sounds from 15 to 20,000 vibrations per second. Dogs and cats can hear sounds as high as 30,000 vibrations per second, and bats can hear 100,000 vibrations per second. At the other extreme are whales and elephants that can hear very low sounds that humans cannot (below 15 vibrations per second).

Extension Activities

Sound Search

In this activity, children use their sense of hearing to find a buddy. Fill pairs of film canisters with equal amounts of the same materials. Use cotton balls, jingle bells, rice, flour, nails, beads, small rubber balls, jacks, toothpicks, sand, dried beans, and so on. Give each child a canister. Tell children not to open up their canisters until you say so. Have children wander about the room, shaking their canisters and listening carefully for a canister that makes the same sound. When they think they have a match, they freeze by their partner until everyone in the room has completed the sound search. Invite students to open their canisters to see if they have the same materials inside as their buddies. Explain that shaking different objects produces different sound waves for our ears to differentiate.

Tap and Blow

Collect identical pairs of glass bottles with narrow openings. Group children so that each group has a pair of bottles with one $\frac{3}{4}$ filled with water and one $\frac{1}{4}$ filled. Instruct children to tap the lower part of the bottles to discover the differences in pitch. Guide them to conclude that the bottle with the most water vibrating produces the lower pitch, and the bottle filled $\frac{1}{4}$ of the way produces the higher pitch. Ask children to predict the results of blowing across the opening of the bottle. (*The pitch is just the opposite.*) Ask children what is vibrating when they tap the bottle (*the whole bottle including the water*), and what is vibrating when they blow across the top (*just the air above the waterline*). This very simple activity helps reinforce the principle of sound that applies to the straw activity, musical instruments, and even to vocal cords: the greater the vibrating mass the lower the pitch.

The Straw Revisited

With practice, your students are probably getting the hang of how to make sounds with the straws they snipped earlier. Ask them to predict what will happen if the straw is cut shorter. After speculating on the results, have them cut their straws in half and blow again. (*The sound will be a higher pitch.*) Predict what will happen if the straw is cut in half one more time. (*The shorter, quicker vibrations cause the pitch to be even higher.*)

✸ Learn More

Books

Bunny's Noisy Book by Margaret Wise Brown (Hyperion, 1999). Bunny wakes up to a world rich with the sounds of birds, roosters, and bumblebees. He experiences his own noises when he munches, stretches, yawns, scratches, and sneezes.

Island in the Sun by Harry Belafonte, Lord Burgess, Alex Ayliffe, and Irving Burgie (Dial, 1999). Celebrate the beauty and culture of Jamaica with calypso.

Little Boy With a Big Horn by Jack Bechdolt (Golden Books, 1999). Ollie's family and neighbors are annoyed when he practices his loud bass horn, until one of his practice sessions saves the day.

The Magic School Bus in the Haunted Museum by Joanna Cole (Scholastic, 1995). Ms. Frizzle's class learns about the science of sound when their bus breaks down on the way to a concert rehearsal. Also available on video.

Sound Experiments (A New True Book) by Ray Broekel (Children's Press, 1983). Simple experiments demonstrate concepts of sound.

Web Sites

Sounds Like Science: Bottle Organ (**www.eecs.umich.edu/mathscience /funexperiments/agesubject/lessons/other /una7.html**): Follow the directions to create homemade musical instruments. Lesson plans cover basic sound concepts.

Neuroscience for Kids: Hearing Experiments (**www.eecs.umich.edu/mathscience /funexperiments/quickndirty/uwash /chhearing.html**): Look for 11 lessons for K–12 teachers on the ear and hearing.

Dirtmeister's Science Lab: Good Vibrations (**teacher.scholastic.com/dirt/index.htm**): Explore the relationship between vibration and pitch.

WebsWiresWaves: The Science and Technology of Communication (**www.eecs.umich.edu /mathscience/funexperiments/quickndirty /webswires/goodvibes.html**): Click on "Good Vibrations" for a "hanger clanger" lesson about what makes sound and how it travels.

Singing Owl Pattern

Mirette on the High Wire

by Emily Arnold McCully (Putnam, 1992)

Young Mirette is scrubbing potatoes in her mother's boarding house when a new boarder, the "Great Bellini," captures her imagination. Bellini is a reluctant teacher, but Mirette is determined to learn his art of walking the high wire. Mirette and the Great Bellini traverse the Paris skyline on a high wire in the climactic scene. For its scenic watercolor portrayal of nineteenth-century Paris, the book won the 1993 Caldecott Medal.

National Science Standards

PHYSICAL SCIENCE

Position and Motion of Objects

❋ The position and motion of objects can be changed by pushing and pulling.

❋ The size of the change is related to the push or pull.

❋ Sharing the Story

To help define *balance*, have students stand up, keeping their hands to their sides. Ask them to bend one leg at the knee. After a few moments ask children to share how it felt to try to balance on one foot without the aid of their arms or other support. Show the cover of the book and discuss what Mirette is doing. Ask: *Why is she holding out her arms?* Have children stand again and balance on one foot. This time invite children to hold out their arms to increase balance. Brainstorm activities that require skill in balancing, such as riding a bike, ice skating, or skateboarding, then share the story.

Science Notes

To understand balance, it is best to start with an understanding of *center of gravity*. The center of gravity is the exact point on an object around which all of the object's weight is evenly distributed. If you alter the weight, the center of gravity changes. Children who balance on a seesaw, for example, naturally work toward adjusting the center of gravity. The center of gravity on a seesaw is at the center of the board when no one sits on it. When two children of different weights sit at opposite ends of the seesaw, the force of gravity will be greater on the end with the heavier child. This will cause the center of gravity to shift from the center of the seesaw to a point between the center and the end that holds the heavier child. As a result the seesaw will tilt toward that end. As children who play on seesaws know, the heavier child can re-establish balance by moving toward the center of the seesaw, which causes the center of gravity to move toward the center again.

Science Vocabulary

gravity: the force that pulls objects toward the center of the Earth

center of gravity: the exact point on an object around which all of the object's weight is evenly distributed

balance: the ability to keep something steady without falling

Balance on Your Finger

MATERIALS

❋ Balancing Toy Pattern (see page 78)

❋ card stock

❋ scissors

❋ jumbo paper clips

1 Photocopy the activity sheet on card stock. Have children carefully cut out the pattern.

2 Tell children to place a paper clip on one of the X's. Let them place the pointed section on the end of their index finger and try to balance the figures.

3 Discuss what happens, then have children place a second paper clip on the other X. Children should find that the high wire duo now balances on their index finger! (Children may have to move the paper clips around a bit to find the balance point.)

SCIENCE TALK

Discuss how the paper clips help balance the toy on their fingers. When children add just one paper clip to the toy, it does not balance because adding just one shifts the pull of gravity to the weighted side. Two paper clips help to rebalance the toy and make it stable on their finger—in the same way that holding out her arms helped Mirette balance on the high wire.

Extension Activities

Balancing Act

This activity puts science at the tips of students' fingers. To make this fascinating toy, each student needs a toothpick that is pointed at both ends and 18 inches of thin-coated wire.

❋ Have students approximate the middle of the wire by simply folding the wire in half so that the ends meet.

❋ Show students how to hold the middle of the wire against the toothpick and wrap one side of the wire around the toothpick with two tight wraps. Then have them wrap the other side of the wire around the toothpick with two tight wraps.

❋ The last step is to have children bend down each side of the wire so that the ends of the wire hang below the toothpick.

❋ Now let the balancing begin. The tip of the toothpick will balance beautifully on the tip of students' fingers as the wire hangs down and lowers the center of gravity. Let them discover that the toothpick will change position as they vary the position of the wire. The difficult part will be getting

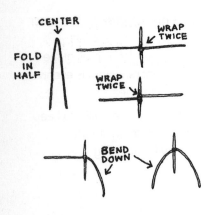

your students to *stop* balancing. Have them put their new balancing toys in bags to take safely home to share with families.

Body Balance

Balance your body! All you need is some wall space. First, ask children to stand by their desks. Have them lift their left foot out to the side and off the floor. (This should be easy for most children.) Now, have them move to the wall and place the side of their right foot and their right shoulder against the wall. Tell them that they must keep their right foot and shoulder pressed against the wall. Invite them try to lift their left foot just as they did a few minutes earlier. Success is impossible! Because they are "glued" to the wall, they cannot adjust their bodies to shift their center of gravity, so they cannot balance on their right foot!

Block Time

When children build a block structure, they naturally employ a cause-and-effect approach to maintain balance within a system and keep the force of gravity from tumbling the structure. Gather a set of blocks and invite teams of builders to take turns building the tallest structure possible. Challenge children to think of block play as building upward against gravity. Discuss ways to maintain balance as the structure rises.

Ideas children may discover to help keep their structures from falling include broadening the base of the structure and keeping heavier blocks at the bottom level rather than up high (to lower the center of gravity).

 Learn More

Books

Barnyard Bigtops by Jill Kastner (Simon & Schuster, 1997). Farm animals join the circus, and Clarence the pig can balance!

High Wire Henry by Mary Calhoun (William Morrow, 1991). Henry the Siamese Cat walks the tightrope to get the attention he craves.

The Napping House by Audrey Woods (Harcourt Brace, 1984). People and animals balance on top of each other like a pyramid.

Web Sites

Davison Community Schools (**www.davison.k12.mi.us**): Enjoy pictures and a balancing quiz from second graders who completed a unit on balance and motion.

Other Resources

Curious George High Wire Act and *Balancing Bear*: These two toys are available at well-stocked toy stores. Hang them up across your classroom on thin string for a balancing act that never ends!

Teaching Physics with Toys by Beverly A. P. Taylor (Terrific Science Press, 1995). This teacher resource contains several activities based on toys that balance.

Balancing Toy Pattern

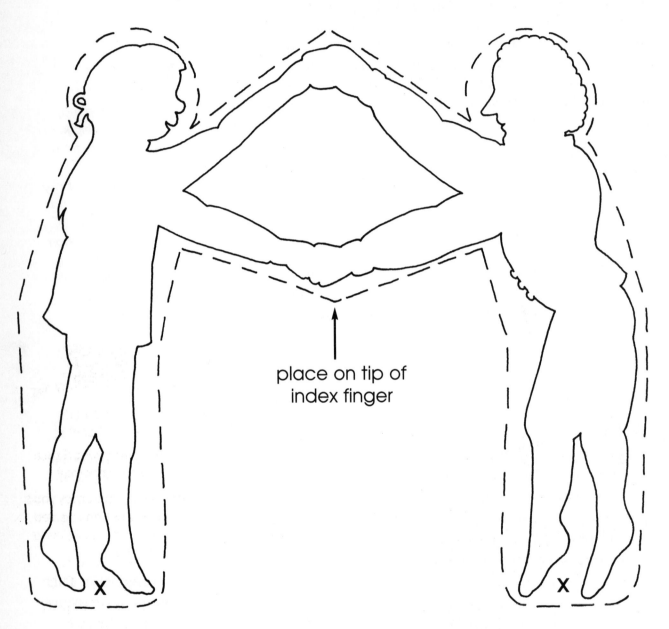

place on tip of
index finger

Teaching Science With Favorite Picture Books Scholastic Professional Books

Pancakes, Pancakes!

by Eric Carle (Picture Book Studio, 1990)

When Jack, a young farm boy, asks his mother for pancakes for breakfast, he doesn't realize all the work that must proceed his meal. From cutting and grinding the wheat for flour, to milking the cow and churning the butter, Jack must start from scratch to gather the ingredients his mother needs to make his breakfast. Children will root for Jack as he grows hungrier and hungrier and finally earns the first buttery bite of his pancake breakfast.

National Science Standards

SCIENCE AND TECHNOLOGY

Understanding Science and Technology

☀ People have always had problems and invented tools and techniques to solve them.

PHYSICAL SCIENCE

Properties of Objects and Materials

☀ Materials can exist in different states, including solid, gas, and liquid.

✿ Sharing the Story

Write the word *pancake* on the chalkboard. Ask children what they notice about this word. (It's made up of two words, *pan* and *cake*.) Let children suggest why pancakes got this name—for example, they are like cakes cooked in a frying pan. Then ask for a show of hands: *Do you like your pancakes to be light and fluffy or flat and rubbery?* Explain that in baking a cake or cooking a pancake the cook needs special ingredients to make it fluffy. As you read the story aloud, have students listen for the ingredients that Jack's mother used to make his pancake. What do they think helps make pancakes fluffy?

Science Vocabulary

carbon dioxide: a gas; it's what makes the fizz when vinegar and baking soda are mixed

ingredients: items in a recipe

technology: science used to make life easier or better

Science Notes

When a *base* (such as the baking soda in pancakes) and an *acid* (such as vinegar) combine, a chemical reaction occurs that produces carbon dioxide. Though the concept of acids and bases is too abstract for young children to grasp, the activities that follow will let them observe chemical reactions between acids and bases that cause changes to occur. Explain that thanks to bubbles like the ones that happen when some acids and bases combine, pancakes can be light and fluffy!

Jack's Flat Pancakes

Whip up two batches of pancakes and taste the difference a little chemistry can make.

MATERIALS

- ✿ chart paper
- ✿ pancake ingredients (see page 83)
- ✿ two mixing bowls
- ✿ mixing spoon
- ✿ electric skillet
- ✿ cooking spray (oil)
- ✿ spatula

1 Label one side of a sheet of chart paper "Jack's Pancakes" and the other "Science Pancakes." Divide each side into three sections labeled "Batter," "Cooking," and "Cooked."

Jack's Pancakes
1 cup flour
pinch of salt
3 tablespoons sugar
1 cup milk
1 egg
¼ cup butter (softened)

Combine the dry ingredients in a large bowl. Place the wet ingredients in another bowl and mix well. Add the wet ingredients to the dry ingredients and mix. Pour pancake batter into a hot, greased skillet (a few spoonfuls for each pancake) and cook over medium heat. Flip pancakes when bubbles form around the edges.

Science Pancakes
2 cups flour
pinch of salt
3 tablespoons sugar
1 teaspoon baking soda

2 eggs
¼ cup vinegar
1¼ cups milk
¼ cup butter (softened)

Combine the dry ingredients in a large bowl. Place the wet ingredients in another bowl and mix well. Add the wet ingredients to the dry ingredients and mix. Pour pancake batter into a hot, greased skillet (a few spoonfuls for each pancake) and cook over medium heat. Flip pancakes when bubbles form around the edges.

2 Mix up a batch of Jack's Pancakes with children. Ask them to describe the mixture. Record comments under "Batter."

3 As the pancakes cook, invite children to describe changes they observe. (*bubbles forming around the edges, the pancakes rising, and so on*) Record comments under "Cooking."

4 Cut pancakes into quarters and share with children. Ask them to describe the pancakes. Record comments under "Cooked."

5 Repeat steps 2 to 4 for the Science Pancakes. As you cut up the pancakes, invite students to notice the bubbles trapped inside. Ask: *What do you think these bubbles are? How do you think they formed?* Try Bubble Up!, below, to find out.

SCIENCE TALK

 Ask children to compare the two recipes on page 83 and identify the ingredients in the Science Pancakes that are not in Jack's. (*baking soda and vinegar*) Focus on the type of ingredients rather than the quantity. (There is more flour, milk, etc. in the Science Pancakes, which is simply to make more batter so that your students have more of these light and fluffy pancakes to enjoy.) Next, let each child discover what made the second batch light and airy by following up your cooking lesson with Bubble Up!, below.

 Extension Activities

Bubble Up!

Try this investigation to let students discover the chemical reaction that occurs in the Science Pancakes. Give each child $\frac{1}{4}$ cup of vinegar in a paper cup and a plastic spoonful of baking soda. When everyone has both ingredients, let children add the baking soda to the vinegar and enjoy watching the bubbles and fizz. Explain that when baking soda is mixed with vinegar a chemical reaction occurs that produces the fizz, or *carbon dioxide gas*. Ask students to use the observations they just made to explain what they think happened to make the bubbles they saw in the Science Pancakes. (*The vinegar and baking soda in the pancake batter created carbon dioxide. As the gas bubbles formed and were trapped in the batter, the pancakes grew bigger and fluffier.*)

Remind children to wash their hands with warm water and soap before beginning this investigation.

Vinegar is generally not used in baking. Instead, other acidic ingredients such as sour cream or buttermilk are mixed with baking soda to produce carbon dioxide. Give students recipe books to browse. Can they find recipes with similar ingredients?

Jack's Butter

Explain that butter sold in stores may have salt added to it for flavor. You might add a little salt to some of your homemade butter so that students can compare unsalted with salted. Take a vote: Which do students prefer?

When Jack needed butter for his pancakes he churned it. Simulate this method of making butter with a science twist. Put a pint of whipping cream into a jar and tighten the lid. Have children sit in a circle and take turns shaking the jar, 10 times each. After about five minutes, a ball of butter will form in the jar. Pour off the liquid and then transfer the butter to a plate. (If you like, you can wrap the butter in cheese cloth and squeeze it gently to wring out any excess liquid.) Spread the butter on crackers or serve it with a second round of pancakes. Let students share how they think shaking cream produced butter. (*Whipping cream contains fat broken into small droplets and dissolved in the milk. Shaking the cream made the fat droplets crash into one another and form bigger and bigger fat drops until one big ball of fat formed—butter! The process in which small drops combine to form bigger drops is called* coalescing. *This is a physical and not a chemical change.*)

 Learn More

Books

Busy Kids Snack Time by Jan Brennan, Lisa Leornardi, Dayle Timmons, and Ann Flagg (The Education Center, 1998). To continue your classroom cooking and chemistry lessons, look here for adorable, no-bake-theme snacks children can make themselves.

If You Give a Pig a Pancake by Laura Joffe Numeroff (HarperCollins, 1989). One in a series of books (*If You Give a Mouse a Cookie*), this book is a fun way to continue the pancake theme.

Pancakes for Breakfast by Tomie dePaola (Harcourt Brace, 1990). This wordless book tells the story of an old woman and the troubles she has as she tries to make pancakes for breakfast.

The Science Chef by Joan D'Amico (John Wiley & Sons, 1994). Children, with a little bit of adult help, will enjoy the experiments, recipes, and projects in this book.

Walter the Baker by Eric Carle (Aladdin, 1998). Find out what happens when a baker substitutes water for milk in this Carle classic.

Video

Magic School Bus: The Ready, Set, Dough (Scholastic, 1997). Travel to a bakery with Ms. Frizzle and her students.

Web Sites

Ooey, Gooey Recipes for the Classroom (**www.minnetonka.k12.mn.us/science/tools /ooey.html**): Learn how to whip up a batch of slime or homemade Silly Putty. There's even a recipe for a singing cake with our favorite ingredient, baking soda!

CafeZOOM (**www.pbs.org/wgbh/zoom/cafe**): Easy-to-make recipes with just a few ingredients will keep excitement cooking in your classroom. Try the Peanut Butter Treats. Students can whip them up in the classroom with just a few ingredients. No baking required!

Pancake Recipes

Jack's Pancakes

1 cup flour

pinch of salt

3 tablespoons sugar

1 cup milk

1 egg

$\frac{1}{4}$ cup butter (softened)

Combine the dry ingredients in a large bowl. Place the wet ingredients in another bowl and mix well. Add the wet ingredients to the dry ingredients and mix. Pour pancake batter into a hot, greased skillet (a few spoonfuls for each pancake) and cook over medium heat. Flip pancakes when bubbles form around the edges.

Science Pancakes

2 cups flour	2 eggs
pinch of salt	$\frac{1}{4}$ cup vinegar
3 tablespoons sugar	$1\frac{3}{4}$ cups milk
1 teaspoon baking soda	$\frac{1}{4}$ cup butter (softened)

Combine the dry ingredients in a large bowl. Place the wet ingredients in another bowl and mix well. Add the wet ingredients to the dry ingredients and mix. Pour pancake batter into a hot, greased skillet (a few spoonfuls for each pancake) and cook over medium heat. Flip pancakes when bubbles form around the edges.

Teaching Science With Favorite Picture Books Scholastic Professional Books

Stone Soup

Retold by Heather Forest (August House Little Folk, 1998)

"Bring what you've got! Put it in the pot!" Your students will chant along with you in this lively version of a familiar folktale. Bright and bold illustrations add interesting details to this story about two cunning and hungry visitors who venture into a mountain village and convince the villagers to pitch in to make a savory pot of "stone soup." Along with a lesson on float-and-sink, this story shares an important life lesson: when each person makes a small contribution, big things can happen!

National Science Standards

SCIENCE AS INQUIRY

Abilities Necessary to Do Scientific Inquiry

✷ Plan and conduct a simple investigation. Communicate investigations and explanations.

PHYSICAL SCIENCE

Properties of Objects and Materials

✷ Objects have many observable properties including size and weight, shape and color, temperature, and the ability to react with other substances.

✷ The position of an object can be described by locating it relative to another object or the background.

Sharing the Story

Before reading the story aloud, give each child a copy of the reproducible. (See page 88.) Let children take turns identifying vegetable ingredients they see. Ask if anyone knows what ingredients are. (*things that go into recipes or other mixtures to make something*) Ask the class to guess what all of these ingredients might make if mixed together. Show the class the cover of the book and then invite everyone to listen to find out how to make stone soup.

Science Vocabulary

sink: an object falls to the bottom of a container

float: an object sits above the water line or hovers between the water line and the bottom of the container

predicting: making reasonable guesses or estimates based on observations or data

Science Notes

What determines if an object will sink or float? Three factors: *buoyancy*, *density*, and *displacement*. Buoyancy is the upward force that liquids exert against an object. Density is an object's mass divided by its volume—the amount of matter in a given amount of space. (An object will sink if its density is greater than the density of the fluid it is in; it will float if its density is less than the fluid it is in.) Displacement is an object's ability to float when it pushes aside—or displaces—a volume of water whose weight is equal to its own. These concepts will be confusing to young children; however, they can grasp the more basic concept that some objects sink in water while others float, and they can use this to build a foundation for later and more complex understandings about buoyancy, density, and displacement.

Sink and Float Soup

Children make sink and float soup with some of the same ingredients that characters in the story shared with the travelers.

MATERIALS

* Sink and Float Soup activity page (see page 88)
* scissors
* a large, clear container
* water
* 1 potato, 1 carrot, 1 stone, 1 stalk of celery, 1 green bean, frozen corn
* glue

Tip

If you have kitchen space available, or can use a crock pot or hot plate, make real stone soup with students. Invite each child to share an ingredient from home (minus the stone). Guide children in preparing the vegetables for cooking. Use water or a vegetable or chicken stock as a base, add vegetables and desired seasonings, then cook and enjoy! Be sure to check for food allergies before serving, and to let the soup cool sufficiently.

1 Give each child a copy of the activity page. Have children cut out the pot and the foods at the bottom of the page.

2 Share the soup ingredients one at a time. Ask students to tell which ones match the pictures.

3 Fill the "pot" (clear container) with water. Hold up the potato and ask children to predict if it will sink or float when placed in the pot. Have them place (but not glue) their potato cutout above or below the waterline on their pot.

4 Invite children to explain their predictions, then have a volunteer "villager" drop the potato into the pot as the class observes what happens. Allow children to move their potato if necessary to match their observations, and then glue it in place. Continue predicting, discussing, testing, and gluing for each ingredient. How many ingredients float? How many sink?

SCIENCE TALK

Use these questions to draw out meaningful observations and age-appropriate conclusions before, during, and after the activity:

☀ *Before we begin let's agree on a definition for floating and sinking. How can we define floating? Sinking?*

☀ *Which objects float? Which objects sink?*

☀ *Do objects that float (or sink) have anything in common?*

☀ *Are sinkers always heavier than floaters?*

☀ *Are floaters always small?*

☀ *Does changing the size or shape of an object make it sink or float? Test it out!*

 Extension Activities

Celery Boats

Celery floats but does that change when it is stuffed with a filling? Give each child a celery stick about three inches long. Float several in water to demonstrate that celery sticks float. Next, have each child design a celery boat using items with which to stuff the celery—for example, peanut butter or cream cheese, and raisins. (You may also use non-food items, such as play clay.) After predicting whether they will sink or float, let children take turns placing their boats in the water. Children will be delighted to see that although their boats may capsize, they will not sink.

Tip

Serve up another round of celery sticks with edible filling but this time eat the ship! Check for food allergies before letting children eat their celery boats.

Sink and Float Crayons

If your class loved making predictions about Stone Soup, try this colorful approach to sink and float. You'll need two boxes of crayons, each from a different crayon company.

✳ Fill a large clear container with water. Make a graph on a large sheet of paper that lists each color and has columns for recording predictions and results.

✳ Open one box of crayons. (Set aside the other box for later use.) Hold up a yellow crayon and ask students to predict whether the crayon will sink or float. Drop the crayon in the water to test the results. Record the prediction (based on a student vote) and result on the graph. Repeat this procedure with other colors, recording predictions and results on the graph.

✳ Repeat the experiment with the second box of crayons, recording results on a new graph. Compare the data gathered on both charts. What generalizations can children make? (Although brands vary, light-colored crayons will usually float while dark crayons will usually sink.)

Now You Know!

The biggest ship in the world is called the Happy Giant. It is a tanker ship that weighs 622,571.5 tons when fully loaded. And it still floats! (Make a connection to the idea that size doesn't determine whether or not something can float by revisiting the results of Sink and Float Soup and the questions in Science Talk.)

Learn More

Books

Keep It Afloat by Julian Rowe and Molly Perham (Children's Press, 1993). This book offers a simple explanation to the sink and float question. *Floating and Sinking* by Jack Challoner (Raintree/Steck Vaughn, 1996) is another good book for teaching this concept.

Red Fox and His Canoe by Nathaniel Benchley (HarperCollins, 1964). Too many friends want to sail in Fox's canoe. How many can it hold before it starts to sink?

Sunken Treasure by Gail Gibbson (Crowell, 1988). This book explores why ships sometimes sink and the different techniques scientists use to recover lost cargo.

Wacky Water Fun with Science: Science You Can Float, Sink, Squirt and Sail by Edwin J.C. Sobey (McGraw Hill, 1999). Take your exploration of floating and sinking further with the demonstrations and experiments in this book.

Web Sites

You Can With Beakman & Jax (**www.beakman.com**): Based on the comic strip of the same name, Beakman's World is packed with wacky science experiments based on questions kids might ask.

Crayola (**www.crayola.com**): If your class is fascinated by the float and sink crayon activity, they may enjoy finding out more about crayons with a tour of the crayon factory and more.

TOPS (**Topscience.org**): Check out some of this commercial curriculum's activities online, including one in which students can observe an ice cube floating on top of cooking oil.

Video

Best of Beakman's World: If your class likes the Beakman web site they will enjoy the video with the same characters.

Sink and Float Soup

potato

corn

stone

carrot

celery stalk

green bean

Teaching Science With Favorite Picture Books   Scholastic Professional Books